Taking Stock of Principal Pipelines

What Public School Districts Report Doing and What They Want to Do to Improve School Leadership

Susan M. Gates, Julia H. Kaufman, Sy Doan, Andrea Prado Tuma, Deborah Kim

RAND CORPORATION

Commissioned by

Wallace™

For more information on this publication, visit www.rand.org/t/RRA274-1

Library of Congress Cataloging-in-Publication Data is available for this publication.
ISBN: 978-1-9774-0526-5

Published by the RAND Corporation, Santa Monica, Calif.

Cover images: Claire Holt/The Wallace Foundation

Preface

The Wallace Foundation commissioned the RAND Corporation to interview district leaders across the country in fall 2019 to broaden understanding about the prevalence of and interest in activities related to principal preparation, hiring, support, and evaluation (referred to as *pipeline activities*). This report presents findings from an interview effort conducted between October and December 2019 to provide a baseline description of principal pipeline activities in districts across the country. It builds on a multiyear evaluation of principal pipelines as described in *Principal Pipelines: A Feasible, Affordable and Effective Way for Districts to Improve Schools* (Susan M. Gates, Matthew D. Baird, Benjamin K. Master, and Emilio R. Chavez-Herrerias, Santa Monica, Calif.: RAND Corporation, RR-2666-WF, 2019). An online appendix, RR-A274-2, provides supplemental material.

We draw on structured interviews with superintendents or senior district officials from a diverse sample of 192 public school districts across the United States. Our findings are intended to be of interest to district and state education agency administrators, principal preservice providers, researchers, The Wallace Foundation, and other K–12 education funders.

This study was undertaken by RAND Education and Labor, a division of the RAND Corporation that conducts research on early childhood through postsecondary education programs, workforce development, and programs and policies affecting workers, entrepreneurship, and financial literacy and decisionmaking. This study was sponsored by The Wallace Foundation, which seeks to foster improvements in learning and enrichment for disadvantaged children and the vitality of the arts for everyone. For more information and research on these and other related topics, please visit its Knowledge Center at www.wallacefoundation.org.

More information about RAND can be found at www.rand.org. Questions about this report should be directed to sgates@rand.org, and questions about RAND Education and Labor should be directed to educationandlabor@rand.org.

Contents

Preface ... iii
Boxes and Figures ... vii
Tables ... ix
Summary ... xi
Acknowledgments ... xvii
Abbreviations ... xix

CHAPTER ONE
Introduction ... 1
Our Interviewees ... 3
Our Questions ... 4
How We Analyzed the Data ... 5
Limitations and Strengths ... 5
Overview of This Report ... 6

CHAPTER TWO
Results ... 7
Nearly All School Districts Reported That School Leadership Is Essential to School Improvement ... 7
Less than Half of School District Respondents Expressed Moderate or High Satisfaction with Their Pool of Candidates for Principal Positions ... 11
What Pipeline Activities Are Most Prevalent? ... 13
Leader Standards for Principals ... 17
Most District Leaders Reported That Their District Used State Leader Standards in Combination with District or Other Standards ... 17
Preservice Preparation ... 19
District Leaders Reported Particularly Striving to Encourage Aspiring Leaders Who Possessed a Range of Less Tangible Skills and Abilities ... 20
District Leaders Provided a Range of Support for Aspiring Leaders ... 21
Of Districts Using Preservice Providers, Majorities Collaborate in Some Way to Support District Needs ... 22

Selective Hiring and Placement 24
Districts Reported Using Multiple Measures and Criteria to Assess Candidates, with Large Districts More Likely to Report Using Performance Tasks 25
On-the-Job Support and Evaluation 26
Districts Use Different Approaches When Supporting Principals 27
The Frequency and Content of Principal Professional Learning in Districts Appeared to Vary Considerably 28
Principal Supervision 29
Who Supervises Principals, and the Number of Principals They Supervise, Varies Widely Across the United States 30
District Pipeline Infrastructure: Leader Tracking Systems and Systems of Support 31
Respondents from Large Districts Were More Likely than Those from Medium Districts to Report Having Offices or Positions Focused on School Leadership 32
Linking Districts' Reported Principal Pipeline Activities with Candidate Pool Satisfaction 32
District Leaders Are Interested in Building Their Pipelines 34
Small Districts Results 37

CHAPTER THREE
Discussion and Conclusions 41

APPENDIXES
A. Data Collection 45
B. Data Analysis 51

ONLINE APPENDIXES
Available for download at www.rand.org/t/RRA274-1
C. Summary of Interview Responses
D. Data Analysis

References 57

Boxes and Figures

Boxes

1.1. The Principal Pipeline Initiative in Six Large School Districts 2
1.2. Why and How We Stratified Our Sample by District Size 3
2.1. What the Six PPI School Districts Were Able to Accomplish 8
2.2. Questions We Asked About the Presence of 11 Pipeline Activities in School Districts 14

Figures

2.1. Percentage of 10K+ Districts Noting Each Focus for District Goals, Plans, or Initiatives Related to School Leadership 11
2.2. Percentage of 10K+ Districts Reporting Prevalence of Principal Pipeline Activities 13
2.3. Percentage of Medium and Large Districts Reporting Prevalence of Principal Pipeline Activities 15
2.4. Percentage of 10K+ Districts Reporting Particular Types of Engagement with Preparation Programs 23
2.5. Percentage of 10K+ Districts Reporting Specific Criteria and Measures to Evaluate Principal Candidates 25
2.6. Percentage of 10K+ Districts Reporting Moderate or Strong Interest in Developing Pipeline Activities 35
2.7. Percentage of Small Districts Noting Presence of Particular Principal Pipeline Activities 38
2.8. Percentage of Small Districts Reporting Moderate or Strong Interest in Developing Pipeline Activities 40

Tables

2.1. Number of Pipeline Activities District Respondents Reported Undertaking 16
2.2. Percentage of 10K+ Districts Reporting Use of State, District, or Other Leader Standards 18
2.3. Percentage of 10K+ Districts Hiring Principals from Preparation Programs with Which They Have Direct Engagement 24
2.4. Percentage of 10K+ Districts Noting Who Coaches and Mentors Principals ... 28
2.5. Pipeline Activities and Satisfaction with Principal Pipeline Among Respondents in 10K+ Districts 33
2.6. Percentage of 10K+ Districts Reporting Particular Barriers to Improving Pipeline Activities 36
A.1. Sample Description 46
B.1. Percentage of 10K+ District Characteristics (Unweighted, Weighted, Population) 53
B.2. Pipeline Activity Estimates for Pipeline Satisfaction Analysis 55

Summary

In this report, we share new learning about the presence and potential importance of principal pipelines for preparing, hiring, supporting, and evaluating school leaders across the United States as reported by administrators from a national sample of school districts. The research on which this report is based was prompted by positive findings in a recent evaluation of the Principal Pipeline Initiative (PPI) conducted by the RAND Corporation and Policy Studies Associates. The PPI, launched by The Wallace Foundation in 2011, supported six large public school districts in implementing comprehensive, strategic efforts intended to improve the quality of school leaders over a five-year period.

The six large urban districts that participated in the PPI made a commitment to enhance their efforts in four main pipeline areas—referred to as *components*—during the PPI:

- **Leader standards:** PPI districts developed or refined leader standards articulating what principals should know and do.
- **Principal preparation:** Districts formed or fostered better partnerships with principal preparation institutions to develop certification programs that focused on district needs or developed or refined principal preparation programs internal to their district.
- **Selective hiring and placement:** Districts worked to make hiring and placement processes for principals more systematic and guided by their leader standards.
- **On-the-job support and evaluation:** Districts improved performance evaluation and access to school leader mentoring and coaching.

As PPI districts worked to connect and support their pipeline activities through efforts that cut across the four areas, the need for three additional activities related to principal supervision and district infrastructure to support those areas became evident:

- Make improvements to **principal supervision**.
- Develop **leader tracking systems** connecting preparation, hiring, support, and/or evaluation.

- Assign responsibility for school leadership issues to a position or office, creating a **system of support** for pipelines.

Thus, although the PPI was initially designed to focus on the first four areas, it evolved to encompass activities in seven areas, or *domains*, over the course of PPI implementation.

Findings from the PPI evaluation (Anderson and Turnbull, 2019; Gates et al., 2019; Kaufman et al., 2017; Turnbull et al., 2016) demonstrated that it was feasible, effective, and affordable for the six districts to implement principal pipelines and that they were able to sustain them after the initiative ended. However, important questions remained about the prevalence of pipeline practices overall and whether principal pipelines make sense for a wider range of districts than those very large urban school districts that were the focus of the PPI.

To begin addressing these questions, we conducted 175 structured interviews from October to December of 2019 with superintendents or other senior officials from a nationally representative sample of public school districts across the country serving 10,000 or more students (*10K+ districts*), along with 17 interviews with superintendents of small districts serving fewer than 10,000 students. Interview questions asked district leaders closed-ended (i.e., yes or no) questions about their satisfaction with their principal candidate pool and 11 specific pipeline activities that map into the seven domains just described.

Leader Standards

1. Does your district **have leader standards** that describe what is expected from school principals?

Preservice Preparation

2. Does your district **have processes or approaches** to encourage school staff to become school leaders?
3. Does your district **give aspiring principals any professional development or support** to become school leaders, either on your own or in collaboration with other organizations such as preparation programs?
4. Does your district **engage with one or more principal preparation programs** on matters relating to how a program is meeting your district's needs?

Selective Hiring and Placement

5. Does your **district use a talent pool process** [i.e., a process of developing a pool of eligible principal candidates] to pre-screen individuals as eligible to apply for principal vacancies in the district?

6. What **criteria** do you use to evaluate and select candidates for principal positions? [Specifically, do respondents mention **performance tasks** as one such criterion?]

On-the-Job Support and Evaluation

7. Are principal **evaluations aligned** to district leader **standards**?
8. Does your district provide **individualized coaching** to all first-year principals?

Principal Supervision

9. Who evaluates (i.e., supervises) principals in your district and how many principals does each supervisor oversee?

District Infrastructure: Leader Tracking

10. Does your district use a computerized **data system** to support decisionmaking about principal hiring, placement, evaluation, and/or support?

District Infrastructure: Systems of Support

11. Does your district have a **position or office** dedicated to school leadership?

In addition to these closed-ended questions, we also asked district respondents open-ended questions regarding the nature of the pipeline activities in which they engaged. We asked about their goals or strategies related to principals, satisfaction with their current pool of principal candidates, and interest in pursuing additional pipeline efforts, as well as barriers to doing so. We used the closed-ended responses to gauge the presence or absence of pipeline activities and analyzed the variation in responses across districts. Because interviewees in all districts confirmed that someone supervises and evaluates principals, our discussion of prevalence focused on the first ten activities for which variation was reported. We analyzed open-ended responses through qualitative coding to better understand pipeline activities across the United States. This report provides a descriptive overview of the features of principal pipelines.

Our report focuses on 10K+ districts, with some comparisons between medium school districts (with 10,000–49,999 students) and large school districts (with 50,000 or more students). We also provide some insights based on the analysis of our exploratory sample of responses from small districts (with fewer than 10,000 students). These small district responses are not representative of the whole population of small districts but may help direct attention to topics worthy of additional research.

Our findings rely on self-reports from senior district leaders who are responsible for district efforts to prepare, hire, and support school principals. Our analysis of response rates suggests the possibility that district officials who were already engaging in or knowledgeable about pipeline activities were more inclined to participate in the interview. It is also possible that respondents provided socially desirable responses to emphasize their work in this area.

Key Findings

In this report, we provide the first-ever national overview of the reported use of and interest in pipeline activities across a wide range of school districts as of the start of school year 2019–2020 as reported by the district officials we interviewed. Our key findings are:

- Ninety percent of respondents from 10K+ districts reported that their district goals, strategic plans, or initiatives tie school leadership to school improvement, suggesting that the district leaders who participated in our study understand the importance of school leadership.
- Less than half of respondents from 10K+ districts reported moderate or high satisfaction with their pool of principal candidates, implying that they see room for improvement in principal pipelines.
- All respondents were able to identify someone responsible for supervising principals, and more than three-quarters of 10K+ district leaders reported having

    - leader standards
    - processes to encourage individuals to be school leaders
    - efforts to give aspiring principals professional development and support
    - standards-aligned evaluation (when they had standards)
    - coaching for all first-year principals.

    Additionally, about half of districts reported actively engaging with at least one principal preparation program and that they used a talent-pool process in principal hiring. It was less common for districts to have a leader-tracking system or a position dedicated to school leadership or to use performance-based metrics in hiring.
- Medium districts were less likely than large districts to report engaging in principal pipeline activities in general; the differences between medium and large districts were statistically significant with regard to having leader standards, having a process to encourage individuals to be school leaders, using performance-based hiring metrics, using standards-aligned evaluation, and having a position dedicated to school leadership.

- Among the ten pipeline activities for which we analyzed variation in prevalence across districts, we found that four were significantly related to respondents' reports of satisfaction with their candidate pool: (1) providing professional development and support for aspiring principals, (2) engaging with at least one principal preparation program, (3) using standards-aligned evaluation, and (4) providing coaching to all first-year principals.
- A majority of respondents expressed moderate or strong interest in improving their district's efforts around leader standards, principal preparation, selective hiring and placement, and on-the-job support and evaluation.
- When asked about barriers to doing more in regard to pipeline efforts, respondents most commonly mentioned lack of time and funding.
- A majority of respondents in our exploratory sample of small districts reported that the superintendent is responsible for principal supervision and that the district is engaged in many of the pipeline activities, including engagement with preservice providers.

Implications

The variation in prevalence of specific pipeline activities reported by our interviewees suggests that there are opportunities for districts to learn from one another. Many districts, especially medium-sized ones, might welcome guidance, examples, and tools that could support them in their strengthening of pipelines. Examples from districts that have been doing such work could inform other districts in their efforts to develop and communicate information about their leader standards, collaborate productively with preservice providers, develop improved criteria for evaluating principal candidates, and create strategies for identifying and improving their pool of principal candidates of diverse ethnicities. Specifically, large districts might be tapped to be models and provide guidance and support to medium and small districts, given that large districts reported a higher level of engagement with pipeline activities.

Districts reported emphasizing on-the-job support and evaluation for principals, but still view it as an area for improvement. Further research is needed to support district decisionmaking by identifying specific approaches or programs that are effective in these areas.

More than 70 percent of respondents overall reported moderate to strong interest in engaging more closely with external preparation program providers. This finding also held for separate categories of large and medium districts as well as our exploratory group of small districts. Preparation programs and state entities that oversee them might think about ways to support meaningful engagement, especially between programs and smaller districts. Research is needed to identify effective collaboration approaches for smaller district and preparation programs.

Responses from officials in small districts suggested some potential differences between small and 10K+ districts in the way principals are supervised and supported; these differences are worthy of further exploration in future research.

Acknowledgments

This report describes insights we derived from 192 interviews with superintendents or other senior district officials. We are extraordinarily grateful to the very busy people who took time out of their schedules to share their insights with us. We also appreciate the assistance we received from other district staff members who helped us identify the appropriate person to interview and scheduled the interviews.

The data-collection effort involved a tremendous team at the RAND Corporation overseen by Deborah Kim and Jennifer Hawes-Dawson. Deborah managed the data-collection effort, including the Institutional Review Board review, pilot test of the interview protocol, recruitment, staffing needs, and interview quality assurance and management. Jennifer designed the data-collection strategy and provided high-level input over the course of the study. Our data-collection team—Garrett Baker, Melanie Borstad, Susannah Faxon-Mills, Katherine Hacthoun, Hanna Han, Ella Henry, Eduardo Lara, Rebecca Lawrence, Nina Ozbardakci, and Chau Phan—recruited participants, conducted interviews, and coded interview data. Garrett also assisted with qualitative interview coding and analysis.

We are also grateful for input we received on the interview protocol design from Brenda Turnbull at Policy Studies Associates, Jevelyn Bonner-Reed of Winston-Salem/ Forsythe County Schools, Mikel Royal at the George W. Bush Institute, Douglas Anthony, Glenn Pethel, and Bronwyn Bevan and Ty Wilde at The Wallace Foundation.

Brian Stecher and Susan Straus of RAND and an anonymous reviewer provided helpful reviews of a draft of this manuscript. Christopher Doss of RAND reviewed the code used to sample districts and analyze the data for this study. Claude Setodji of RAND advised on the sampling, and Lou Mariano of RAND provided advice on the weighting approach.

Ninna Gudgell carefully edited the original manuscript and created the figures and text. Linda Theung carefully edited the final copy, and Monette Velasco efficiently managed the production of the final report.

The authors take full responsibility for any remaining errors.

Abbreviations

FRPL	free or reduced-price lunch
LEA	local education agency
LEP	limited English proficiency
NCES	National Center for Education Statistics
PD	professional development
PLC	professional learning community
PPI	Principal Pipeline Initiative
PSEL	Professional Standards for Educational Leadership
SRG	RAND Survey Research Group
TA	technical assistance

CHAPTER ONE

Introduction

In 2011, The Wallace Foundation launched the Principal Pipeline Initiative (PPI). Over five years, the PPI would support six large, urban public school districts in implementing comprehensive, strategic efforts intended to improve the quality of school leaders. Findings from the PPI evaluation (Anderson and Turnbull, 2019; Gates et al., 2019; Kaufman et al., 2017; Turnbull et al., 2016) demonstrated that it was feasible, effective, and affordable for the six districts to implement principal pipelines and that the districts were able to sustain them after the initiative ended (see Box 1.1). The studies found that schools with newly placed principals in PPI districts outperformed comparison schools from other districts in the state in student achievement and principal retention. This evidence of success has drawn the attention of district and state leaders around the country to the concept of principal pipelines. However, important questions remain about the prevalence of principal pipeline activities and whether principal pipeline activities make sense for a wider range of districts than those large districts that were the focus of the PPI. In particular, it is unclear whether a strategic focus on principal pipeline activities would make sense for smaller school districts with many fewer principal positions to fill each year.

In this report, we share findings from interviews conducted with senior officials from a national sample of school districts across the United States about the presence and potential importance of principal pipelines and the priority that districts place on developing or improving them. The study focused on the following research questions:

- To what extent do U.S. school districts view school principals as a key lever for school improvement?
- Are district administrators satisfied with their current pool of candidates for principal vacancies?
- To what extent do district administrators report having mechanisms and strategies for preparing, hiring, supporting, and retaining principals?
- What is the level of interest in developing or improving those strategies?
- What barriers do district leaders report to implementing mechanisms and strategies for preparing, hiring, supporting, and retaining principals?

Box 1.1. The Principal Pipeline Initiative in Six Large School Districts

The six large urban districts that participated in the PPI made a commitment to enhance their efforts in four main pipeline areas:

- **Leader standards:** PPI districts developed or refined leader standards articulating what principals should know and do.
- **Principal preparation:** Districts formed or fostered better partnerships with principal preparation institutions to develop certification programs that focused on district needs or developed or refined principal preparation programs internal to their district.
- **Selective hiring and placement:** Districts worked to make hiring and placement processes for principals more systematic and guided by their leader standards.
- **On-the-job support and evaluation:** Districts improved performance evaluation and access to school leader mentoring and coaching.

As PPI districts worked to connect and support their pipeline activities through efforts that cut across the four areas, they also

- made improvements to **principal supervision**
- developed **leader tracking systems** connecting preparation, hiring, and support and/or evaluation
- assigned responsibility for school leadership issues to a position or office, creating a **system of support** for pipelines.

In other words, over time, the PPI evolved to encompass activities in seven areas or "domains" over the course of PPI implementation.

The findings from the PPI evaluation suggest that, when districts adopt a strategic approach to these activities, it can make a difference for schools and students in terms of student achievement and can improve principal retention. These findings have prompted district and state officials to consider pipeline activities as a lever for school improvement. Yet researchers, policymakers, and district leaders have valid questions about the extent to which these strategies are already being used and whether they are potentially attractive to districts smaller than those in the PPI.

For more information about the PPI—its implementation, effects, and sustainability—see Anderson and Turnbull, 2019; Gates et al., 2019; Kaufman et al., 2017; and Turnbull et al., 2016.

To address these questions, we conducted 175 structured interviews from October to December 2019 with superintendents or other senior officials from a nationally representative, stratified random sample of public school districts across the country serving 10,000 or more students (we call them *10K+ districts* in this report). Box 1.2 describes why and how we stratified our sample by size. These 10K+ districts included both medium districts serving 10,000–49,999 students and large districts serving more than 50,000 students. We also conducted 17 interviews with superintendents or senior officials of small school districts serving fewer than 10,000 students. Interviewees were located in 41 states in school districts serving as few as 200 students to more than 600,000 students.

We provide a brief overview of our research methods in this report, including the design of our interview protocol, the people we spoke with, and decisions we made about how to select the sample of district respondents. The appendixes of this report provide more details about our sample, the data-collection procedures, and our methods of analysis.

Our Interviewees

We spoke with superintendents or other senior district officials knowledgeable about district efforts to prepare, hire, and support school principals in 192 school districts. Our interviewees included 55 superintendents; 88 associate, assistant, or area superintendents;[1] and 74 leaders with other titles, such as executive director, chief, or

Box 1.2. Why and How We Stratified Our Sample by District Size

The size distribution of school districts in the United States is highly skewed. There are more than 13,000 school districts in the country, and more than 12,000 of these are small districts that serve fewer than 10,000 students. On average, each small district serves fewer than 2,000 students; altogether, these districts educate more than 21 million students. Because large districts have been the focus of research to date on principal pipelines and pipeline activities, we stratified our sample to prioritize data collection from districts serving 10,000 or more students but included small districts in our sample in a more limited way.

[1] The titles of seven associate, assistant, or area superintendents emphasized leadership, and 15 titles emphasized human resources or talent management.

director.[2] In 15 cases, we talked with more than one person in a single district interview. In those cases, we recorded a single response for the district. Any reference to district respondents in this report refers to the collective responses for these 15 cases and not individual interviewees. Our overall response rate was 23 percent. This response rate reflects hard refusals as well as nonresponses or inabilities to complete the interview within the short data-collection window.

The 175 10K+ district respondents were somewhat more urban, served fewer white students, and served more free or reduced-price lunch (FRPL)–eligible students than 10K+ districts nationwide. We used survey weights to further improve the extent to which the 10K+ respondent sample matches the population of 10K+ districts on select student enrollment characteristics. We then used the survey weights to develop the weighted average responses presented in this report. See Appendix B for more details about the sample characteristics and weighting.

Our Questions

We used a structured interview protocol to gather information about the following topics of interest efficiently and systematically:

- the extent to which the district views school principals as a key lever for school improvement
- district satisfaction with the current pool of candidates for principal vacancies
- whether the district is engaged in specific pipeline activities to prepare, hire, support, and retain principals and the nature of their engagement in these activities
- the level of interest in specific pipeline activities and perceived barriers to implementing them.

The protocol included closed-ended questions that were limited to a yes, no, or categorical responses and a more-limited number of open-ended questions to gather richer information from district respondents about what these pipeline activities look like on the ground, the level of interest in enhancing key pipeline activities, and what barriers they perceive to implementing these activities. It was designed be completed in 20–30 minutes. We made a conscious effort to limit the use of jargon from the PPI while addressing the core concepts of that effort. The interview protocol and approach were reviewed and approved by the RAND Corporation's Institutional Review Board.

---

[2] The titles of 19 of these interviewees emphasized leadership, and 27 title emphasized human resources or talent management.

How We Analyzed the Data

Responses to open-ended question were categorized using predefined codes reflecting expected themes. These codes were refined in the first several weeks of interviews based on topics discussed in the interviews. Interviewers conducted all the coding of open-ended responses, and two researchers deeply familiar with principal pipelines double coded 11 percent of the interviews to assess and ensure coding reliability. Any substantial disagreements in the coding were discussed and resolved at weekly meetings with all interviewers and the research team; these meetings were also a chance to make any necessary updates to the coding plan and the coding itself.

We weighted average responses to close-ended questions and open-ended responses that were coded and quantified for the 10K+ districts. We generated and analyzed tabulated responses for two key subgroups of the weighted 10K+ sample: medium districts (those serving 10,000–49,999 students) and large districts (those serving 50,000 or more students). We also generated tabulations of unweighted responses from small districts to support an exploratory analysis. Finally, we used a regression model that accounted for some district-level factors to examine whether the reported presence or number of specific pipeline activities was associated with the likelihood of reported satisfaction with the principal candidate pool.

Limitations and Strengths

Our national estimates reflect findings based on 175 responses from 10K+ districts (i.e., excluding the 17 responses from small districts). These findings rely on self-reports from senior district leaders who are responsible for district efforts to prepare, hire, and support school principals. Because the findings from the PPI evaluation have generated some attention in the press and professional organizations in the education field, it is possible that respondents provided socially desirable responses that emphasize their work in this area, even if their efforts are relatively minor.

Concurrent with the interview effort, The Wallace Foundation was supporting technical assistance (TA) on principal pipelines for school districts around the country (which is a separate effort from the Wallace-funded PPI that took place from 2011 to 2016). All large districts were invited to participate in the TA, and about one-half chose to do so. The Wallace Foundation also invited some medium districts to participate in the TA effort. Our study *included* all large districts in the country, regardless of whether they chose to participate in the TA.[3] At the request of The Wallace Foundation, we

[3] Among the 175 10K+ districts that responded, roughly 40 were affiliated with The Wallace Foundation through the TA, PPI, or University Principal Preparation Initiative. Descriptively, Wallace-affiliated districts reported rates of pipeline activity usage higher than 10K+ districts overall, but similar rates to districts of comparable size.

excluded from our study medium districts that chose to participate in the TA out of concern about the potential burden that participation might pose for these smaller districts.[4] This means that our sample of medium districts is potentially biased away from districts with the greatest interest in pipeline activities. Our response rate was 23 percent overall and varied by district size category and TA participation (see Table A.1 in Appendix A and the related discussion). The response pattern suggests a possibility of unobservable response bias in our sample, with district officials in larger districts and those participating in the TA potentially being more favorably inclined toward or more knowledgeable about principal pipeline activities.

Despite these limitations, this report provides a first-ever national overview of the use of and interest in pipeline activities across a wide range of school districts as of the start of school year 2019–2020 as reported by the district officials we interviewed.

Overview of This Report

In the next chapter, we present key results organized around the seven areas of pipeline activities described in Box 1.1. In the third and final chapter, we discuss the results and offer conclusions. Two technical appendixes provide additional information about our data-collection and data-analysis approaches (Appendix C, Summary of Interview Responses; Appendix D, Principal Pipeline Baseline Interview Instrument). Supplemental material consisting of tabulations of interview responses and the interview instrument are available for download at www.rand.org/t/RRA274-1.

---

[4] Thirty-five out of 821 medium districts were excluded on this basis.

CHAPTER TWO

Results

In this section, we summarize key findings based on district administrators' responses about their perceptions of the importance of school leaders, their satisfaction with their districts' pool of school leaders, and the prevalence of pipeline activities in their districts. We then provide a more in-depth examination of district leaders' perceptions of activities and needs related to the seven groups of pipeline activities. Box 2.1 summarizes what the PPI districts were able to accomplish to provide a basis for interpreting the survey findings in this report.

Overall, the vast majority of our interview participants across districts reported that their district views principals as important and engages in some pipeline activities. That said, only about half of district respondents reported that they are satisfied with their current pool of principals. Interviewees reported some of the pipeline activities to be far more prevalent than others. In addition, our data suggest variation in what principal pipelines look like in different district contexts.

We emphasize findings from the full sample of 10K+ districts, unless otherwise noted. Where relevant, we highlight statistically significant differences between average weighted responses for two subgroups of 10K+ districts: medium districts (those serving 10,00–49,999 students) and large districts (those serving 50,000 or more students). We augment our results with data and quotes from coded responses to open-ended questions. At the end of the results section, we describe responses from 17 leaders in small districts who participated in our interviews. Small district responses are considered exploratory and are not weighted.

Nearly All School Districts Reported That School Leadership Is Essential to School Improvement

Research has documented the important role that school principals can play in school improvement and the effect of principal characteristics and behaviors on key outcomes (see, for example, Béteille, Kalogrides, and Loeb, 2012; Grissom and Loeb, 2011; Grissom, Mitani, and Woo, 2018; Harvey and Holland, 2013; Liebowitz and Porter, 2019; Louis et al., 2010). To understand more about how school districts view school

Box 2.1. What the Six PPI School Districts Were Able to Accomplish

Our interview protocol was structured to gather information about the extent to which senior district officials in school districts around the country view their own district as engaged in and/or interested in the pipeline activities that the six PPI districts focused on. For more information about the PPI and its implementation, effects, and sustainability, see Anderson and Turnbull, 2019; Gates et al., 2019; Kaufman et al., 2017; and Turnbull et al., 2016.

Leader Standards

All districts participating in the PPI adopted district-specific leader standards that served as a guide for all aspects of their principal initiatives—from hiring criteria to principal professional development and evaluation. Furthermore, PPI districts revisited their standards frequently, both to ensure that the standards reflected elements of leadership that they felt were important in their context and to ensure that their preparation, hiring, support, and evaluation processes were well aligned with those standards.

Preservice Preparation

All PPI districts undertook activities to align principal preparation with their leader standards and their expectations for the principalship. That said, PPI districts took considerably varied approaches to principal preparation—from developing and sustaining their own in-house principal preparation administrator certification programs (often including residencies) to working closely with local preservice providers. The costs of these efforts varied substantially among PPI districts (Kaufman et al., 2017).

Selective Hiring and Placement

All PPI districts worked to make hiring and placement much more systematic by ensuring that these activities align closely with leader standards and provide objective data on leader skills and experiences. The use of objective data for hiring contrasts with a heavy reliance on interview data or personal relationships to assess skills and experiences of candidates. By the end, all PPI districts were using talent pools to pre-screen candidates for principal vacancies, and many districts were using performance tasks or other assessments of capabilities as part of that process.

Box 2.1—Continued

On-the-Job Support and Evaluation

All PPI districts made considerable effort to improve principal on-the-job support and align that support with their evaluation systems. The PPI districts focused on the provision of support in the first several years after a principal was hired into the position. The support that was offered to principals varied from district to district, but each provided at least some mentoring and coaching, along with regular trainings, aligned with their leader standards.

Principal Supervision

Five of the six PPI districts also worked to reduce the span of control—the average number of principals—under the supervision of any one person in the district.

Infrastructure (Leader Tracking Systems)

All PPI districts developed data systems—called leader tracking systems—designed to support improved preparation, hiring, and support of school leaders.

Infrastructure (Systems of Support)

In all the PPI districts, some resources were directed toward systems and infrastructure to support pipelines. For example, PPI district staff focused specifically on leadership issues, sometimes with a specific office of leadership where all that work took place.

leadership, we asked school district leaders the following questions at the start of our interviews:

- Do your district's goals, strategic plans, or initiatives tie school leadership to school improvement?
- How do these goals, strategic plans, or initiatives focus specifically on improving preparation, hiring, support, and/or evaluation of school principals?

Responses to the latter, open-ended question were qualitatively coded to determine whether responses suggested a focus on preparation, hiring, support, and/or evaluation.

Findings suggest that 10K+ district leaders regarded school leadership as a key aspect of school improvement. Ninety percent of 10K+ district leaders in our study indicated that their district's goals, strategic plans, or initiatives indeed tied school leadership to school improvement.

When asked to elaborate on how those goals, strategic plans, or initiatives focused on principal preparation, hiring, support, or evaluation, most respondents (88 percent) mentioned specific district activities focused on at least one of these categories of pipeline activities. As indicated in Figure 2.1, according to our qualitative coding, more than half of interview respondents in 10K+ districts mentioned a focus or initiative related to on-the-job support for principals. Between one-quarter and one-third of respondents mentioned a focus on some aspect of principal preparation, including programs to support emerging leaders or those seeking administrator certification, improving the hiring and selection of principals, or improving evaluation processes or principal evaluation scores (see Table 29 in the supplemental material). Nearly half of the respondents (42 percent) in large districts said that their district had goals, plans, or initiatives specifically focused principal preparation, which was significantly higher than the 26 percent of medium districts focused on principal preparation. We did not find other significant differences between medium and large districts in the pipeline focus.

Most district respondents discussed school leadership as one of numerous foci for their district, sometimes noting the importance of cultivating strong staff, including principals and teachers. A smaller number districts specifically called out leadership as their main focus. Our qualitative data illustrate some of the ways in which districts described how their districts prioritize school leadership and balance it with other goals:

> Our district mission talks about a community, which includes staff, students, parents, and leadership. Our annual goals vary by year. . . . Our school leaders are generally on the top of that list. We rely on them to make sure that initiatives work well.

> I think, for the district, it's a core value. We see our principals as executive leaders. Our investment in them is a priority.

> Our goals are primarily student achievement goals. We have other goals that are set by the district that may be more operational. Principals are hired and expected to achieve student achievement goals.

> There's an objective and a priority in our goal on operation effectiveness around talent and retention and hiring. That's about all employees, but it includes school principals.

> [W]e believe there is a direct link to strong leadership and student outcomes. In looking at our scorecard, our students are first and foremost [when it comes to] providing the absolute best education. And through that, we believe having strong leaders in place makes the difference.

Figure 2.1
Percentage of 10K+ Districts Noting Each Focus for District Goals, Plans, or Initiatives Related to School Leadership

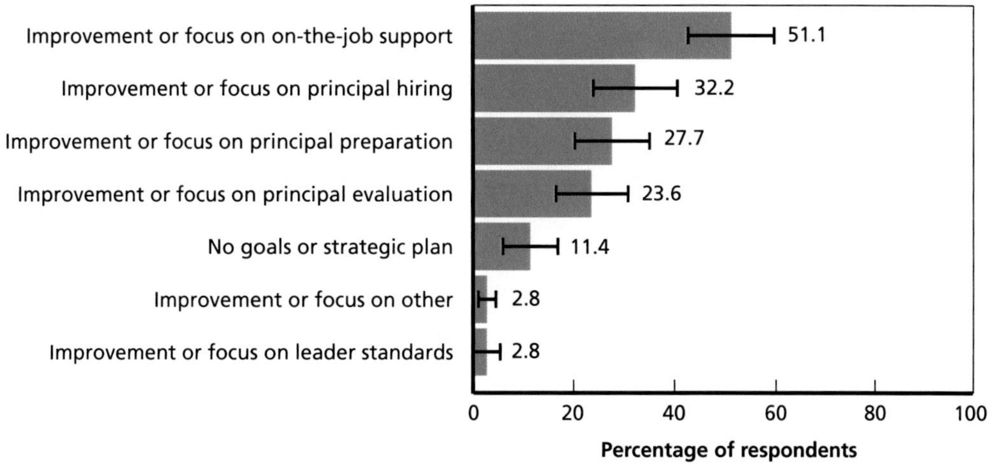

NOTE: Bars reflect weighted survey data from respondents in 10K+ districts indicating that their district's goals, strategic plans, or initiatives indeed tied school leadership to school improvement (n = 159). Error bars represent 95-percent confidence intervals.

Less than Half of School District Respondents Expressed Moderate or High Satisfaction with Their Pool of Candidates for Principal Positions

After asking school leaders about how they emphasized school leadership in their overall district goals, we asked them the following questions to gauge their satisfaction with their principal candidate pool:

- How satisfied are you with the pool of candidates available to fill principal vacancies in your district in terms of principals' demographic background and competencies? Would you say very dissatisfied, dissatisfied, neither dissatisfied nor satisfied, satisfied, or very satisfied?
- Thinking about the available pool of candidates to fill principal vacancies in your district, what gaps, if any, do you see?

Responses to the latter, open-ended question were qualitatively coded to categorize gaps that came up in the interviews (e.g., gaps in principals of specific ethnicities or genders, gaps in principals with specific soft skills).

Although respondents reported that school leadership was critical to school improvement and other district priorities, only 49 percent of 10K+ districts reported being moderately or highly satisfied with the pool of candidates for principal positions. This is somewhat consistent with findings from a survey of superintendents reported by Davis (2016), in which 80 percent of respondents described a need for improvements to principal preparation programs.

Based on qualitative coding of our data, district respondents most frequently noted a lack of candidates (see Table 30 in the supplemental material)

- from specific ethnic groups (48 percent)
- with leadership experience (34 percent)
- with particular leadership skills (33 percent).

Many who brought up particular leadership skills referred to instructional leadership, including deep understanding of standards, curriculum, and pedagogy among leaders. A smaller number of respondents referred to the need for leaders to have social and interpersonal skills, such as being able to advise teachers and have hard conversations with them, as well as engage with parents and the community. Respondents less often named other skills, such as the ability to set a vision, manage change, and build a positive school culture. The frequent mention of the need for more principal candidates with instructional leadership skills reflects the growing recognition that such skills are key to supporting teaching and learning, which was also reflected in meta-analyses noting the relationship between student achievement and such leadership actions as supporting the development and use of curriculum, instruction and assessment or planning, and coordinating and evaluating teaching and curricula (Copeland and Neely, 2013; Herman et al., 2017; Leithwood et al., 2004; Marzano, Walters, and McNulty, 2005; Robinson, Lloyd, and Rowe, 2008).

Several respondents identified leader diversity as a gap in the principal candidate pool. One leader described strategies her district is using to address the challenges:

> Our district has about 85 percent students of color. . . . Currently, we have more white leaders than we have leaders of color. . . . Historically, in our city, we have not fulfilled our diversity quotas at the teaching level. Most of our leaders rise up, from either the classroom or have been teachers . . . so there has always been a shortage of teachers and leaders, so that inhibits a natural pipeline for leaders of color. One of the things we are addressing is recruitment and what that might look like. So we have been talking about reaching out to historically black colleges to engage in not just leaders but teachers as well. We are in the initial stages. We have a group to design and carve out these opportunities.

Having established that districts view school leadership as important and that many are not fully satisfied with their candidate pool, we now consider how school districts across the United States perceive, engage with, and prioritize aspects of principal pipelines studied as part of the PPI. We first consider the pipeline activities that appear to be most prevalent in 10K+ districts across the United States and then provide more detail about responses related to leader standards, principal preparation, selective hiring and placement, on-the-job evaluation and support, principal supervision, and district infrastructure (including leader tracking systems and offices or positions focused on principal leadership).

What Pipeline Activities Are Most Prevalent?

We asked respondents structured (i.e., typically closed-ended) questions designed to help us understand whether the district was engaged in 11 specific pipeline activities. Box 2.2 describes the questions and their relationship to the seven pipeline areas.

Figure 2.2 summarizes the reported prevalence of ten of the 11 activities described in Box 2.2 across the country for the 10K+ districts (excluding the ninth activity on

Figure 2.2
Percentage of 10K+ Districts Reporting Prevalence of Principal Pipeline Activities

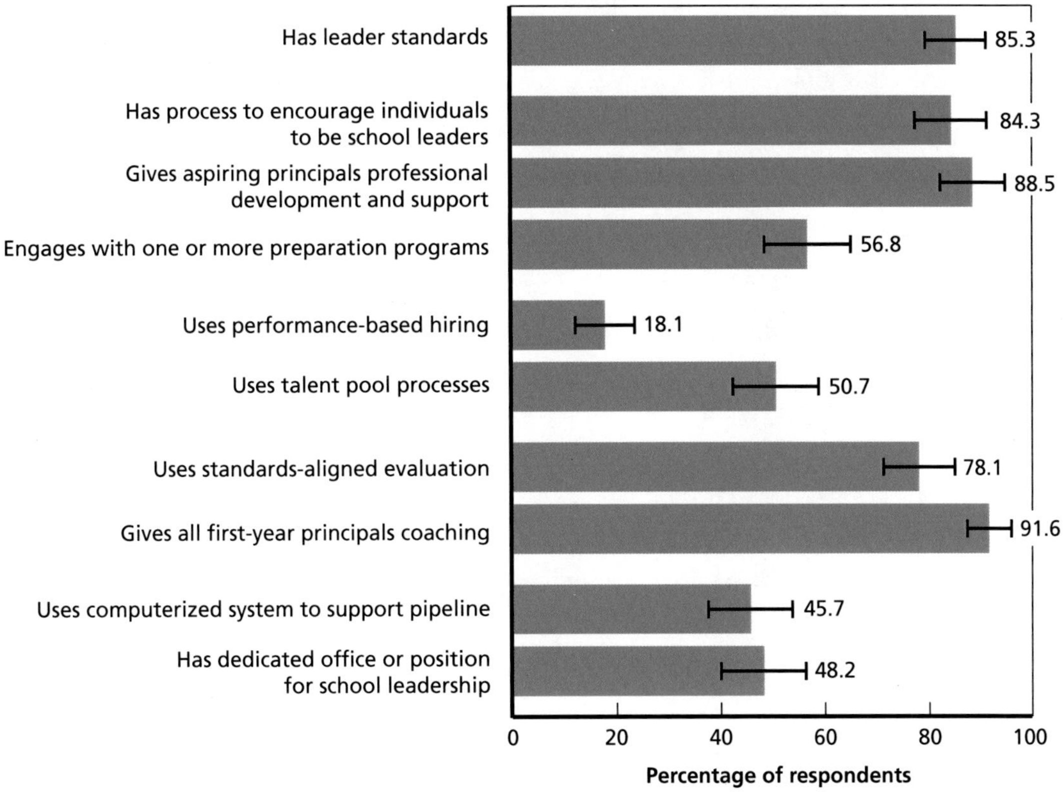

NOTE: Bars reflect weighted survey data from respondents in 10K+ districts (n = 175). Error bars represent 95-percent confidence intervals.

Box 2.2. Questions We Asked About the Presence of 11 Pipeline Activities in School Districts

Leader Standards

1. Does your district have leader standards that describe what is expected from school principals?

Preservice Preparation

2. Does your district have processes or approaches to encourage school staff to become school leaders?

3. Does your district give aspiring principals any professional development or support to become school leaders, either on your own or in collaboration with other organizations such as preparation programs?

4. Does your district engage with one or more principal preparation programs on matters relating to how a program is meeting your district's needs?

Selective Hiring and Placement

5. Does your district use a "talent pool" process to pre-screen individuals as eligible to apply for principal vacancies in the district?

6. What criteria do you use to evaluate and select candidates for principal positions? [Specifically, do respondents mention performance tasks as one such criteria?]*

On-the-Job Support and Evaluation

7. Are principal evaluations aligned to district leader standards?

8. Does your district provide individualized coaching to all first-year principals?

Principal Supervision

9. Who evaluates principals in your district, and how many principals does each supervisor oversee?*

District Infrastructure: Leader Tracking Systems

10. Does your district use a computerized data system or systems to support decisionmaking about principal hiring, placement, evaluation and/or support?

District Infrastructure: Systems of Support

11. Does your district have an administrative position or office dedicated to school leadership?

* *Question was open-ended; responses were qualitatively coded.*

supervision).[1] Figure 2.3 shows how the prevalence of each activity differed between medium and large districts. The vast majority of 10K+ districts reported having leader standards, having a process to encourage individuals to become a school leader, giving aspiring principals professional development and support, using standards-aligned evaluation (when they have standards), and providing coaching to all first-

Figure 2.3
Percentage of Medium and Large Districts Reporting Prevalence of Principal Pipeline Activities

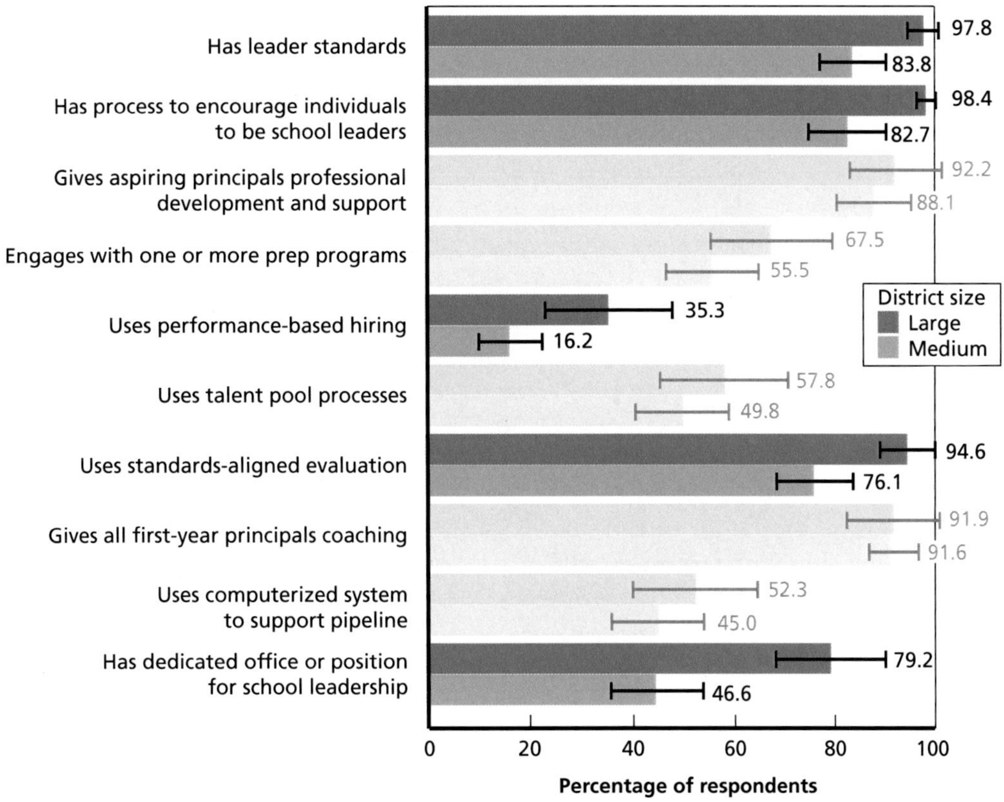

NOTE: Bars reflect weighted survey data from respondents in medium districts (*n* = 130) and large districts (*n* = 45). Error bars represent 95-percent confidence intervals. Dark bars and labels for medium and large districts indicate that the differences for that item are statistically significant at the $p < 0.05$ level.

---

1 "Uses performance-based hiring" was identified through responses to an open-ended question about the factors that districts consider in principal hiring. We also asked district respondents to tell us who (or what position) was responsible for evaluating principals and the number of principals such people oversaw. As respondents in all districts were able to identify the person responsible for principal's supervision, we do not report on prevalence in the charts (Principal Pipeline Activity #9). We elaborate on district leaders' responses about who supervises principals and the number of principals supervised and focus on what respondents said about principal on the job support and evaluation later in this report.

year principals. About half of districts reported that they actively engage with at least one principal preparation program or use what is typically referred to as a "talent pool process" to pre-screen individuals as eligible to apply for principal vacancies in the district. Less than half of 10K+ districts had one of the infrastructure elements we examined, with 46 and 48 percent of districts reporting that their district had a computerized system and dedicated school leadership office or position, respectively.

Figure 2.2 also separates responses related to the prevalence of pipeline activities for medium and large districts. Medium districts were less likely than large districts to report engaging in principal pipeline activities in general. The differences between medium and large districts were statistically significant on having leader standards, having a process to encourage individuals to be school leaders, using performance-based hiring metrics, using standards-aligned evaluation, and having a position dedicated to school leadership.

We tabulated the number of principal pipeline activities that individual districts said they were undertaking, with the view that districts that engaged in more of these activities might be thinking about or developing a more-comprehensive pipeline to support improvements to the principalship. Table 2.1 shows all the districts that reported engaging in at least three activities—99 percent reported engaging in at least four and 85 percent reported engaging in six of the 11 pipeline activities. Only about 3 percent of 10K+ districts indicated engaging in all 11 activities.

Table 2.1
Number of Pipeline Activities District Respondents Reported Undertaking

Number of Pipeline Activities	Percentage of 10K+ Districts	Percentage of Medium Districts	Percentage of Large Districts
At least 1	100	100	100
At least 2	100	100	100
At least 3	100	100	100
At least 4	99	99	100
At least 5	92	92	94
At least 6	85	84	94
At least 7	68	65	92
At least 8	55	52	79
At least 9	34	31	60
At least 10	11	8	32
All activities (11)	3	1	14

SOURCE: Analysis based on RAND interview responses.
NOTE: Using a Kolmogorov-Smirnov test, we found that the distributions of the number of pipeline components used by medium and large districts differed at the $p < 0.05$ level.

Findings from the PPI evaluation suggest that the number of principal pipeline activities in which districts report engaging might not be as consequential for improving school leadership as the depth and quality with which districts engage in pipeline activities that are most critical to their own contexts (Gates et al., 2019).

Having summarized district leaders' reports about the overall prevalence of pipeline activities, we provide more-detailed information about the variation in prevalence and characteristics of activities in key groups of pipeline activities: leader standards, principal preparation, selective hiring and placement, on-the-job evaluation and support, principal supervision, and district infrastructure.

Leader Standards for Principals

As we just noted, the bulk of leaders in 10K+ districts that we spoke with indicated that their district had standards that described what is expected of principals. Large districts were more likely to report having leader standards compared with medium districts (97 percent versus 84 percent).

Principal Pipeline Activity #1

Does your district have leader standards that describe what is expected from school principals?

Response: Eighty-five percent of 10K+ district leaders said yes.

In addition to asking about leader standards, we also asked districts that reported having such expectations whether those standards were developed and adopted by the state, district, and/or other organization.[2] Finally, we asked districts an open-ended question about how leader standards were communicated to principals in their district, responses to which were qualitatively coded.

Most District Leaders Reported That Their District Used State Leader Standards in Combination with District or Other Standards

Leader standards establish a district's expectations for those who assume the role of principal, including their performance in the role. The standards can serve as a starting point for efforts to improve other pipeline activities (Turnbull et al., 2016). Although

2 The National Policy Board for Educational Administration released the Professional Standards for Educational Leadership (PSEL) in 2015 as an update to 2008 standards released by the Interstate School Leaders Licensure Consortium. These standards articulate goals for school leader practice in everything from setting mission, vision, and core values to creating conditions that ensure equity to supporting professional community for teachers and staff. Many states have adopted either PSEL or state school leader standards, and both can serve as guides for districts.

districts can develop standards from scratch, there are starting points at the national and state level. PSEL, a new set of national researcher-based standards for principals, was released in 2015 (National Policy Board for Educational Administration, 2015). All states have adopted state leader standards, which, in many cases, are aligned to national standards (Scott, 2018).

Our interview data suggest that districts are leveraging these national and state standards resources. Eighty-five percent of 10K+ districts indicated using state-level standards; fewer districts reported having locally developed district leader standards instead of or in addition to their state leader standards. Roughly one-third of our sample indicated having adopted other leader standards, which they often noted were the national standards (i.e., PSEL) and occasionally standards derived from evaluation rubrics, such as Marzano or Danielson (for more information, see Danielson Group, undated; Marzano, undated).

Among 10K+ districts that had leader standards, about 30 percent indicated using state-sourced leader standards *only*. It was more common for districts to report using leader standards from a combination of sources; roughly 60 percent of districts reported using leader standards derived from a combination of state, district, and/or another source. Of those with leader standards, we found no significant differences in the usage of state, district, or other leader standards between medium and large districts (Table 2.2).

Among districts that reported using standards, nearly all 10K+ district respondents indicated that these standards were communicated to school principals. Sixty-five percent indicated they were communicated through principal evaluation or coaching and 63 percent indicated communicating them through professional development opportunities, while 18 percent indicated communicating them through onboarding or induction periods (see Table 31 in the supplemental material).

Table 2.2
Percentage of 10K+ Districts Reporting Use of State, District, or Other Leader Standards

	District Size Category	
Source of Leader Standards	**Medium (Percentage)**	**Large (Percentage)**
State	85	85
District	58	60
Other	35	28

NOTES: Percentages calculated based on weighted survey data from respondents in medium (n = 111) and large (n = 44) districts that reported having standards. Columns do not sum to 100 because some districts reported more than one source for leader standards.

Preservice Preparation

Prior research on principal preservice preparation has focused on limitations in principal preparation programs (Briggs et al., 2013; Davis, 2016; Manna, 2015). These limitations could have implications for the quality of candidates for principal vacancies within districts. But research also emphasizes the important role that districts can play in improving preparation through collaborations with principal preparation programs to both identify promising candidates and inform program design (Darling-Hammond et al., 2007, Wang et al., 2018).

To assess how much district leaders were doing in the area of principal preparation, we examined what the districts reported doing to both encourage and cultivate existing staff to be leaders and to collaborate with preservice providers. The vast majority of district respondents (upward of 85 percent) indicated that their district had processes or approaches to encourage school staff to become leaders and provided professional development and support to aspiring principals. Nearly all of the respondents in large districts (98 percent) noted such processes, whereas 83 percent of those in medium districts did. However, just a little more than half of the respondents told us that they engaged with at least one principal preparation program about how that program is meeting districts' needs.

To dig deeper into the ways in which U.S. school districts are supporting and influencing principal preparation, we also asked district respondents the following combination of close-ended and open-ended questions; responses to the open-ended questions were qualitatively coded:

Principal Pipeline Activity #2

Does your district have processes or approaches to encourage school staff to become school leaders?

Response: 84% of 10K+ district leaders said yes.

Principal Pipeline Activity #3

Does your district give aspiring principals any professional development or support to become school leaders?

Response: 88% of 10K+ district leaders said yes.

Principal Pipeline Activity #4

Does your district engage with one or more principal preparation programs on matters relating to how a program is meeting your district's needs?

Response: 57% of 10K+ district leaders said yes.

- Does your district have processes that intentionally strive to encourage individuals with particular characteristics and experiences to become school leaders? Would you say yes or no?
- What particular leadership characteristics or experiences is your district especially interested in promoting?
- How does your district engage with principal preparation programs [If the district reported engagement]?
  - About program course content?
  - About leader standards?
- Does your district keep records of the preparation programs providing administrative certification that your principals completed?
- Do any principals in your district come from administrative certification programs your district has direct engagement with? If so, can you estimate the proportion that do so?

District Leaders Reported Particularly Striving to Encourage Aspiring Leaders Who Possessed a Range of Less Tangible Skills and Abilities

As just noted, 85 percent of respondents said they had processes in their district that encourage any individuals to be school leaders. Respondents in 69 percent of both medium and large districts also noted having processes that encourage individuals with specific characteristics to becomes school leaders.

When asked about the types of skills, characteristics, and experiences their districts were particularly interested in promoting, respondents in 10K+ districts mentioned a wide range of skills and abilities (see Table 34 in the supplemental material). Some district leaders brought up the need for specific leadership skills, as they did when asked about gaps in particular characteristics of leadership candidates. Others brought up a wide range of skills and abilities they look for in those that they might encourage to be school principals, including some that might be considered less immutable characteristics in individuals. Some representative examples include the following:

> We are looking for someone who is self-aware and results-driven, service oriented to our community and is able to enact high expectations. Someone who is interpersonal, can communicate effectively, and is able to collaborate effectively. Someone with courage and a positive work ethic who is committed to equity and is able to instill trust in their division and organization. Someone who can ensure a positive climate and culture, makes great decisions, and can remain focused on stakeholders, students, and [the] community instead of what is important for them.

> We look for innate characteristics, like dynamic and charismatic personalities, strong work ethic, people with the capacity to be very conceptual in nature and see the big picture, but also be able to manage . . . we look for people who can connect very fluently with the community . . . people who are really able to understand and

look closely at their school needs and data [and] be able to create a solid action plan for continuous improvement.

Only 10 percent of respondents mentioned race, ethnicity, or gender when describing the particular leadership characteristics or experiences their district was especially interested in promoting. This was somewhat surprising, given that 48 percent of respondents indicated a lack of principals of specific ethnicities when probed about gaps in their principal candidate pool.

District Leaders Provided a Range of Support for Aspiring Leaders

More than 88 percent of respondents from 10K+ districts indicated that their district provided some kind of professional development or support for aspiring principals within their district. Of these, more than three-quarters mentioned that their district directly provided professional development focused on leadership (78 percent), while 38 percent indicated that their district provided support for aspiring principals to attend externally provided professional development or training (see Table 35 in the supplemental material). We heard about numerous training opportunities and support for aspiring leaders, including trainings focused on developing teacher leaders to professional learning opportunities for those specifically interested in the principalship (for both teachers and assistant principals). Some of the responses reflect the range of opportunities available across districts:

> We do an aspiring teacher leader program, an aspiring administrator program, and a teacher leader institute. We start at the campus level by promoting going into the teaching field with our high school students and have programs for that. Once we get aspiring leaders in the classroom, we see them taking on roles and just being available and willing to work hard and collaborative in their PLCs [professional learning communities].

> Our division also has an aspiring principal's academy, which is for assistant principals. . . . We also have a leadership development training for teachers who want to be administrators. . . . We have a number of principals [who] conduct their own mini-principal academies because they are committed to the division and interested in the development of the folks [who] work for them. They might meet with five or six teachers that express an interest once a week or once a month.

We did not ask respondents how they selected aspiring leaders for programs and opportunities, although some volunteered that they nominated or chose teachers to attend, whereas others implied that any interested teacher could choose to attend a given opportunity.

Of Districts Using Preservice Providers, Majorities Collaborate in Some Way to Support District Needs

As noted, 58 percent of 10K+ district respondents in our study reported that they engage directly with at least one principal preparation program. We hypothesized that more-extensive engagement and collaboration would be relatively rare and—when observed—be more common in large districts because they hire more principals and may have more central office capacity to support such engagement (Wang et al., 2018). However, the differences we observed between medium and large districts were not statistically significant. Among the districts that reported engagement with preparation providers, only about one-quarter described surface-level communication that did not delve into how programs could meet district needs, whereas more than half described genuine collaboration and communication about how preparation programs could meet district needs, with no differences in those reporting collaborations to meet district needs in medium and large school districts (see Table 36 in the supplemental material). Furthermore, many districts described the cadence of meetings between districts and preparation programs as frequent and regular. For example, one of our respondents from a medium district remarked that some district staff serve on a preparation program's advisory board, confer with them "quite often" regarding district needs, and have formal annual meetings to review those needs and discuss future plans. In another example, a respondent from a large district noted that they meet "routinely" with their university preparation program partners:

> [The preparation programs] are always wanting to partner and get people into their programs. We normally ask members of our staff to teach some of those classes and make sure that we have some flexibility in the curriculum to make sure we teach our future administrators the way we do things in our district . . . it's a collaboration; we understand they have goals and they understand our needs to have the program aimed at things we are doing.

We specifically asked districts that reported engagement with principal preparation programs about whether that engagement focused on preparation program content or leader standards (see Tables 14 and 15 in the supplemental material). Sixty-six percent of leaders in 10K+ districts reported interacting with preparation course content, and 58 percent reported engaging with their leader standards. On both items, we found that large districts were more likely than medium districts to engage in these specific forms of collaboration with preparation programs (see Figure 2.4). In fact, all respondents in our sample from the largest districts (those serving 99,000 students or more) indicated that they directly collaborated with preparation programs on these topics.

This level of direct engagement about content and standards with preparation programs among large districts might be because respondents from large districts were more likely than those from medium districts to hire principals from programs with which they have the closest contact (Table 2.3). Specifically, among those who

Figure 2.4
Percentage of 10K+ Districts Reporting Particular Types of Engagement with Preparation Programs

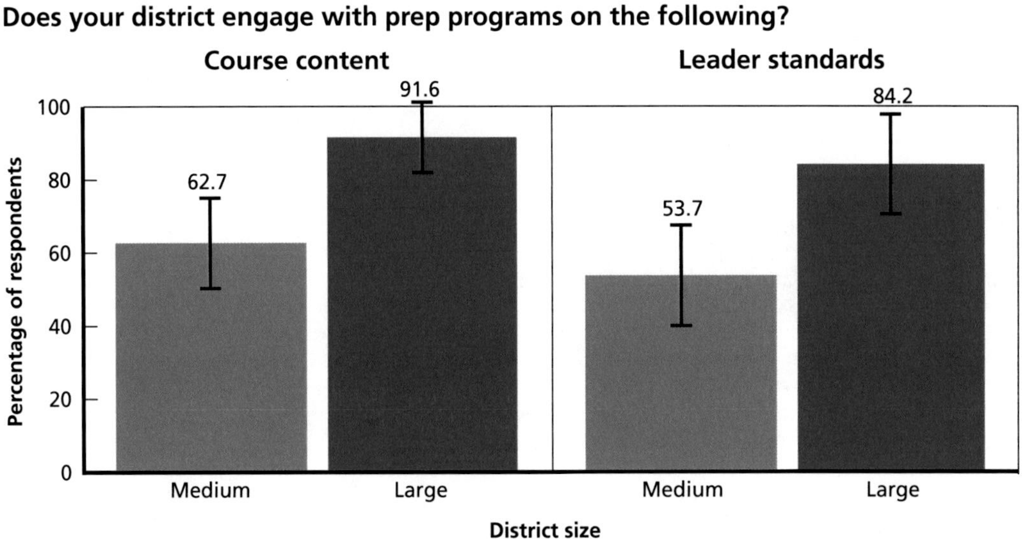

NOTE: Course content bars reflect weighted survey data from respondents in medium (n = 75) and large (n = 31) districts that reported some engagement with preparation programs. Leader standards bar reflect weighted survey data from respondents in medium (n = 67) and large (n = 29) districts. Error bars represent 95-percent confidence intervals.

reported tracking the programs that their principals participated in, large districts were significantly less likely than medium districts to have hired no principals from a preparation program with which they have engaged (7 percent versus 25 percent). Nearly 60 percent of large districts that tracked their principals' preparation information hired at least half of their principals from a partner preparation program.

Selective Hiring and Placement

All school districts that employ principals face a need to fill a principal vacancy at some point in time. Large districts that employ dozens or even hundreds of principals need to fill multiple vacancies each year. Smaller districts may have more periodic needs. Education research has identified a handful of observable characteristics of principals, such as experience as a teacher in the same school and experience as a principal or assistant principal more generally, that are associated with school outcomes (Bowers and White, 2014). But there is limited research about principal hiring practices and their effectiveness, and little evidence links objective characteristics of candidates, such as years of teaching experience or advanced degrees, to success on the job (see Herman et al., 2017). Clifford (2010) highlighted some innovative practices that districts were

Table 2.3
Percentage of 10K+ Districts Hiring Principals from Preparation Programs with Which They Have Direct Engagement

	District Size Category	
Percentage of Principals in District Hired from Program	**Medium**	**Large**
No principals	25	7
> 0–50 percent of principals	51	36
> 50 percent of principals	23	58

NOTE: Percentages calculated using weighted survey data from respondents in medium (n = 83) and large (n = 37) districts that reported that they "keep a record of the preparation programs providing administrative certification that your principals completed." Respondents reporting that that no principals in their district came from administrative certification programs that their district has had direct engagement with are coded as "no principals." Available response options for districts reporting that they have hired at least one principal from an administrative certification program that their district has had direct engagement with include (1) 0–5 percent, (2) 6–10 percent, (3) 11–25 percent, (4) 26–50 percent, (5) more than 50 percent, (6) don't know, and (7) refuse. Respondents who answered "don't know" or "refuse" are treated as missing.

pursuing to make hiring more strategic by aligning it to standards and using multiple measures, including performance-based measures based on simulation or role-play. For example, candidates might be asked to give a presentation to a group of teachers about strategies for improving student outcomes, and their performance would be assessed against a structured rubric by trained raters (Wildy, Pepper, and Guanzhong, 2011). PPI districts implemented candidate screening strategies in their hiring processes to create "talent pools" of high-quality candidates eligible for open principal positions and reported that such pools were useful (Turnbull et al., 2019).

Principal Pipeline Activity #5

Does your district use a talent pool process to prescreen individuals as eligible to apply for principal vacancies in the district?

Response: 51% of 10K+ district leaders said yes.

Principal Pipeline Activity #6

What criteria do you use to evaluate and select candidates for principal positions? [Specifically, do respondents mention performance tasks as one such criteria?]

Response: 18% of 10K+ district leaders said yes.

Our interviews explored the hiring and placement practices of districts across the United States in our sample. Although substantial majorities of district leaders in our study indicated having leader standards and processes to support preparation of aspiring principals, lower percentages indicated engaging in the principal pipeline activities that we associated with systematic hiring and placement. Specifically, only about half of districts reported using a talent pool process, with no significant differences between medium (50 percent) and large (58 percent) districts. Less than 20 percent reported using performance tasks as criteria for hiring.

To gather more details on principal hiring processes, we asked respondents to describe what criteria their district used to evaluate and select principals. Figure 2.5 summarizes our qualitative coding of the responses to this open-ended question, which touched on both measures they used for assessing principal candidates (e.g., interviews, community feedback) and criteria (e.g., standards, prior experience).

Districts Reported Using Multiple Measures and Criteria to Assess Candidates, with Large Districts More Likely to Report Using Performance Tasks

Although most respondents described using multiple measures and criteria to assess candidates, the most commonly cited assessment measure, by far, was candidates' responses to interview(s) (55 percent). The most common criteria that district leaders mentioned were prior teaching or leadership experience (44 percent) and school fit (40 percent). Importantly, we have evidence that districts used assessments that included

Figure 2.5
Percentage of 10K+ Districts Reporting Specific Criteria and Measures to Evaluate Principal Candidates

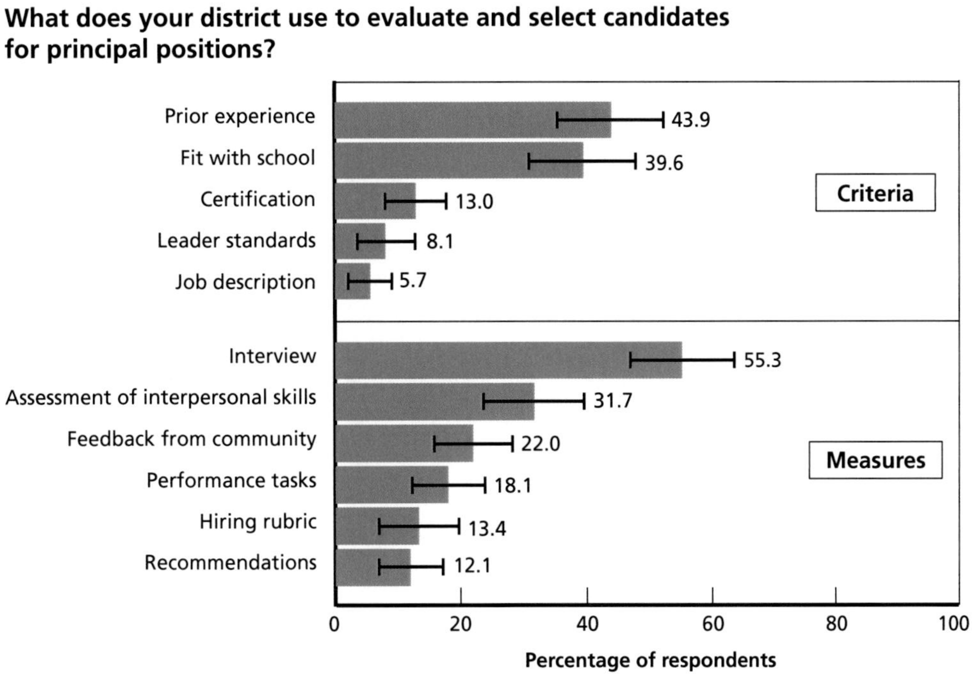

NOTE: Bars reflect weighted qualitative code data from respondents in 10K+ districts (n = 175). Error bars represent 95-percent confidence intervals.

performance-related sources of information: 32 percent mentioned assessments of interpersonal skills, 18 percent used performance tasks, and 13 percent reported having a hiring rubric. It should be noted that respondents brought up these criteria and measures without being prompted; some respondents might have neglected to mention everything they do to evaluate candidates (e.g., interviews likely take place most of the time but only 55 percent mentioned them as the criteria they use to evaluate and select candidates).

Our data suggest that there may be some differences in assessment methods and criteria that districts of different sizes rely on to evaluate principal candidates (see Table 38 in the supplemental material). For example, 35 percent of respondents from large districts reported using performance tasks to evaluate principal candidates, compared with 16 percent of those in medium districts. In contrast, 46 percent of those in medium districts cited leadership or teaching experiences as important criteria, compared with 29 percent in large districts.

Districts' descriptions of their hiring approaches show variation in complexity and comprehensiveness of school principal hiring processes across the United States. Some respondents noted simpler processes, such as this description from a respondent from a large district: "We do a paper screening, a personal interview, and reference checking." Other district leaders described a much more comprehensive process, such as this response from another interview from a respondent in a large district:

> We start with a paper screening to make sure that they have the appropriate certifications and years of experience. Once they fit that criteria, they have a face-to-face interview. Once they are successful at that level, they are moved to the pool, and they have a superintendent staff interview to be put into the principal pool. Once you [sic] are in the pool, you have a panel interview with school administrators, parents, teachers, classified personnel, and the associate superintendent, and they screen everyone in the pool who is interested in that particular school. We are trying to gauge what candidates know about professional learning communities, instruction, data analysis, team building, planning and assessment, dealing with challenging discipline problems, and employees, employee growth, and communication. . . . We also have a writing sample, with prompts based on real-life scenarios. We are looking at open-ended question and real-world interview responses.

On-the-Job Support and Evaluation

In the preservice preparation section of this report, we noted ways in which districts reported supporting aspiring leaders. We now consider how districts described their principal support and evaluation efforts. Districts can support productive professional growth of school principals through constructive evaluation using multiple measures that, in turn, inform targeted on-the-job support (Aguilar, Goldwasser, and Tank-Crestetto, 2011; Guilfoyle, 2013). Although there is some research providing suggestive evidence about the characteristics, leadership styles, and actions of principals that are associated with desirable outcomes for schools and students, only two professional development programs have demonstrated evidence of success (see Herman et al., 2017).

Between 80 and 90 percent of district respondents in our sample indicated that both their district used an evaluation that aligned with their leader standards and all first-year principals received individualized coaching or mentoring.

Principal Pipeline Activity #7

Are principal evaluations aligned to district leader standards?

Response: 78% of 10K+ district leaders said yes.

Principal Pipeline Activity #8

Does your district provide individualized coaching to all first-year principals?

Response: 92% of 10K+ district leaders said yes.

We asked the following additional closed- and open-ended questions to ascertain how principals were supported and evaluated within school districts:

- What proportion of principals in your district receive individualized coaching or mentoring? (All/none/some)
- Who provides the coaching and mentoring?
- Is the principal coaching and mentoring based on individual needs, evaluation, and/or other factors?
- Other than coaching or mentoring, in what other ways does your district support professional learning for principals?

Districts Use Different Approaches When Supporting Principals

Virtually all 10K+ districts indicated that they provided individual coaching to at least some of the principals in their district, with roughly 60 percent of these districts reporting that they provided individualized coaching or mentoring to all principals in their district. Among districts providing coaching to only some principals, the vast majority (85 percent) reported that they provided individual coaching or mentoring to all first-year principals, but only 25 percent indicated that their district provided coaching to all principals in their second and third year. Only 2 percent of respondents across 10K+ districts indicated that principal coaching was being provided to all principals with more than three years of experience. Seventy percent of districts indicated that they provided individual coaching to at least "some" principals with two or more years of experience.

When asked about whether coaching was based on individual needs or evaluation, virtually all respondents indicated that these visits were to address the "individual needs" of each principal, implying that the coaching was targeted rather than general. Fewer respondents (65 percent) stated that these visits were informed by needs identified in evaluation.

Interview responses provide some additional information about how districts structure coaching and mentoring (Table 2.4). A key tension in the field has been whether coaching or mentoring is integrated with or separate from evaluation (Goldring et al., 2018; Lochmiller, 2018). Roughly 80 percent of respondents indicated that individuals in supervisory roles (i.e., those who evaluate the principals) also coach or mentor principals (see Table 40 in the supplemental material). Among those that indicated that supervisors provided coaching or mentoring, more than two-thirds also indicated that another person, in addition to the principal supervisor, within or outside their district provided additional coaching or mentoring to principals. Those "others" who might also provide principal coaching or mentoring included other district employees, individuals, or organizations outside of the district and—in some cases—retired school or district leaders. Coaching or mentoring was provided only by someone other than the principal supervisor in about 20 percent of districts.

The Frequency and Content of Principal Professional Learning in Districts Appeared to Vary Considerably

About half of the respondents (49 percent) indicated that their district provided training to principals, and more than one-third (40 percent) said that principals in their district attend meetings that include a support or professional learning component (see Table 41 in the supplemental material). Yet the frequency and content of principal

Table 2.4
Percentage of 10K+ Districts Noting Who Coaches and Mentors Principals

Role	Percentage of 10K+ Districts Reporting Involvement in Principal Coaching and Mentoring
Principal supervisor only	27
Supervisor and nonsupervisor	52
Nonsupervisor only	21

NOTE: Table created using weighted qualitative code data from respondents in 10K+ districts who indicated providing individualized coaching or mentoring to at least some principals in their district (*n* = 171).

meetings within districts appeared to be quite variable. For example, although many respondents reported monthly principal meetings, some mentioned bimonthly or even weekly meetings. Furthermore, although nearly all respondents who cited district principal meetings said that they included some support component, many also said that the meetings could also focus on operational or administrative concerns to varying degrees. For example, in one medium-sized district, a respondent described monthly administrative meetings where principals receive "very specific training related to district initiatives and/or the tools that either they're being asked to use or teachers are being asked to use." Another respondent said that, at principal meetings, they try to maintain a 50-50 split between professional learning and providing principals with administrative information. Still other respondents reported that principal meetings were primarily focused on professional learning. About one-third of respondents specifically described meetings as PLCs. A few respondents even noted that their district had evolved somewhat to focus more on professional learning for principals as opposed to more-operational and administrative concerns. Some examples include the following:

> [W]e've spent so much energy to provide increasingly relevant and sustained PD [professional development] for teachers that we're turning around in central office saying we should be doing the same. We've converted our monthly meetings from agenda to training, modeling what we'd be doing in the classroom, sharing.

> We have principal meetings for colleagues on the same level. This is evolving to be more of a PD focus, where they are identifying their own topics and planning their days based on their identified growth areas.

Beyond district principal meetings and PLCs, more than one-third (38 percent) of respondents also reported providing funding to support principals' pursuit of training or further education on their own outside of the district. Those opportunities could range from principal institutes and retreats offered by outside organizations to national and state leadership conferences.

Principal Supervision

Research conducted by the Council of the Great City Schools in 2012 concluded that districts needed to focus more attention on principal supervision (Corcoran et al., 2013). Among the recommendations from that research was a call to narrow the set of responsibilities of principal supervisors to focus on principal development and the span of control. The term *span of control* is used to describe the number of individuals directly reporting to one manager or supervisor. Although organizations seek guidance about the right target, that number is likely influenced by context, including tasks typically assigned to a supervisor, differences in needs of direct reports, and other factors (Acharya et al., 2017). In the case of principal supervisors, context likely includes not only tasks that supervisors are typically assigned but also the geographical location of principals and the types of schools they serve.

Building on this research, The Wallace Foundation encouraged districts participating in the PPI to focus attention on principal supervision. The foundation launched a separate initiative—the Principal Supervisors Initiative—to support such efforts in six other districts. Evaluation studies documented the success of participating districts in shifting the role of principal supervisors and reducing the span of control (Anderson and Turnbull, 2019; Goldring et al., 2018; Turnbull et al., 2016).

Principal Pipeline Activity #9

Who evaluates principals in your district and how many principals does each supervisor oversee?

Response: All district leaders identified one or more principal supervisors.

We asked the following questions to learn more about principal supervision within school districts:

- Who is the direct supervisor that evaluates the principals in your district?
- How many principals does (this person/each person) typically supervise?

Who Supervises Principals, and the Number of Principals They Supervise, Varies Widely Across the United States

The average number of principals supervised by any one individual as reported by 10K+ district respondents in our study was 14. But respondents reported that district administrators could be supervising anywhere from three to 40 principals. The reported average number of principals being supervised by one person was 13.5 for medium districts and 18.4 for large districts. The reported average increased with the size of the district, with the average for the districts serving 10,000–19,999 students being about five principals, whereas the average for districts serving more than 99,000 students was about 21 principals (see Table 45 in the supplemental material).

In addition to the variation in the number of principals supervised, we found variation in who was responsible for supervising principals and conducting their evaluations. In medium districts, principals were more likely to be evaluated directly by the superintendent, whereas this evaluation role shifted to assistant superintendents or other district administrators (e.g., executive directors, area directors, academic officers) in large districts.

District Pipeline Infrastructure: Leader Tracking Systems and Systems of Support

District infrastructure could support development of comprehensive principal pipelines (Anderson, Turnbull, and Arcaira, 2017). We asked about two elements of district infrastructure that might be relevant to principal pipelines: data systems that might support leader tracking and a dedicated office that addresses school leadership.

Principal Pipeline Activity #10

Does your district use a computerized data system or systems to support decisionmaking about principal hiring, placement, evaluation, and/or support?

Response: 46% of 10K+ district leaders said yes.

Principal Pipeline Activity #11

Does your district have an administrative position or office dedicated to school leadership?

Response: 48% of 10K+ district leaders said yes.

Less than half of respondents from 10K+ districts reported that their district used a computerized data system of some kind to track principal hires, placement, evaluation, or support, and a similar share reported having a position or office dedicated to school leadership.

We asked the following additional questions to learn more about the way data systems were being used.

- What type of computerized data system(s) does your district use to get input or gather data to improve school leadership?
- How does your district use the data system(s)?
- Would a computerized data system used to track hiring, placing, and evaluating school principals be useful to your district? Would you say yes or no?

Respondents from Large Districts Were More Likely than Those from Medium Districts to Report Having Offices or Positions Focused on School Leadership

There were no significant differences between the responses from medium and large districts about whether the district uses a computerized data system or systems to support decisionmaking about principal hiring, placement, evaluation, and/or support. But respondents in large districts were more likely than those in medium districts to report that their districts had an individual or position dedicated to school leadership (see Figure 2.2). Among respondents from large districts, 79 percent reported that they had a position dedicated school leadership, compared with 45 percent of respondents from medium districts.

The most common types of data systems reported by respondents from 10K+ districts include those for tracking principal support or evaluation (60 percent) and tracking principal applicants and hires (45 percent). Only 7 percent of respondents mentioned data systems that bring together data on principal hiring, placement, support, and/or evaluation. When asked how they used data systems, a majority of respondents indicated using one for a single purpose (e.g., principal hiring or evaluation). Only 17 percent mentioned using a data system or systems for more than one purpose (e.g., hiring *and* evaluation). When asked how these data systems were used, district officials' responses matched the types of data systems they indicated having. Respondents most commonly mentioned using the system to track evaluation data (55 percent) and principal candidates background, skills, and experience for hiring purposes (40 percent). A smaller percentage of districts mentioned using the system to predict principal vacancies (14 percent) or to track principal participation in professional learning opportunities (8 percent).

Linking Districts' Reported Principal Pipeline Activities with Candidate Pool Satisfaction

When we asked respondents to indicate the extent to which they were satisfied with their current pool of candidates to fill principal vacancies, only 49 percent of districts indicated that they were either satisfied or very satisfied. We were curious about whether the reported presence or number of specific pipeline activities was associated with the likelihood that respondents indicated that they were satisfied or very satisfied with their principal candidate pool. To explore this association, we used a regression model that accounted for some district-level factors (Table 2.5).[3]

Among the ten pipeline activities, we found that four were significantly related to district satisfaction: (1) providing PD and support for aspiring principals, (2) engaging

[3] Regression models accounted for district size, district student race and ethnicity composition, district percentage of FRPL-eligible students, district percentage of limited English proficiency (LEP) students, the presence of "focus" or "priority" schools in the district, and district urbanicity. See Appendix B for more information.

Table 2.5
Pipeline Activities and Satisfaction with Principal Pipeline Among Respondents in 10K+ Districts

Component	Percentage of 10K+ Districts	Significant Predictor of Satisfaction
Leader standards		
District has leader standards	85	
School leader preparation		
District has process to encourage individuals to be school leaders	84	
District gives aspiring principals PD and support	88	✓
District engages with at least one preparation program	57	✓
Selection hiring and placement		
District uses talent pool	51	
District uses performance-based hiring	18	
Support and evaluation		
District uses standards-aligned evaluation	78	✓
District gives all first-year principals individual coaching	92	✓
Infrastructure		
District uses computerized system to support principal pipeline	46	
District has dedicated office or position for school leadership	48	

SOURCE: Analysis based on RAND interview responses. $p < 0.05$ used as the level of statistical significance reported in the table.

with at least one preparation program, (3) using standards-aligned evaluation, and (4) providing all first-year principals with individual coaching. In all these significant cases, the size of the association between the presence of that activity and respondent satisfaction was large. For example, respondents indicating that their districts offered PD and support for aspiring principals were 35 percentage points more likely to be satisfied with their current candidate pool. Similarly, the presence of engagement with preparation program(s), standards-aligned evaluation, and first-year principal coaching was associated with 18, 25, and 31 percentage point increases in the likelihood of satisfaction, respectively.[4] Conversely, self-reports of the presence of the seven other

[4] Additional details and regression coefficients for results presented in Table 2.5 are available in Table B.2 in Appendix B.

activities listed in Table 2.5 were not significantly related to the probability that respondents reported that they were satisfied with the state of their principal pipelines.

Although the results presented in Table 2.5 offer some suggestive evidence about a relationship between the reported use of certain pipeline activities and satisfaction with the principal candidate pool, these findings should be interpreted with caution for a number of reasons. The measures of both the presence of pipeline activities and pipeline satisfaction rely on self-reports from senior district officials. A district official's perception of principal pipelines may be unrelated, or only weakly related, to empirical indicators of pipeline success (e.g., principal competencies, student outcomes, principal retention). In addition, responses about the implementation of particular pipeline activities may have been under- or overstated. Where responses were accurately stated, our data-collection approach provided limited opportunities to assess the quality of that implementation. Lastly, although we were able to control for some observable district characteristics, additional factors could confound the relationships we identified above (e.g., wealthier districts may be more likely to provide professional development for aspiring principals and have advantages unrelated to professional development that result in higher quality principal pipelines). Studies capable of measuring pipeline activities more precisely using administrative and other forms of data and relating specific activities or combinations of activities to outcomes of interest could improve our understanding about whether certain pipeline activities are more important than others and whether engaging in more activities drives better outcomes.

District Leaders Are Interested in Building Their Pipelines

After asking district leaders about the work they were doing to support each area of the principal pipeline explored in this report, we asked them questions to ascertain their interest and ability to do more in each of these areas. Specifically, for each pipeline area examined in our interview—leader standards, principal preparation, selective hiring and placement, on-the-job support and evaluation, and infrastructure—we asked the following:

- How interested are you in doing more to improve [in this pipeline activity]? No interest/slight interest/moderate interest/strong interest
- What factors might keep your district from doing more [in this pipeline area]?

Figure 2.6 summarizes the responses to these questions. These responses could inform efforts by state actors and other third-party organizations interested in supporting district pipeline efforts.

Most of those in our district sample communicated interest in improving aspects of their principal pipelines. Three-quarters or more of the district respondents

Figure 2.6
Percentage of 10K+ Districts Reporting Moderate or Strong Interest in Developing Pipeline Activities

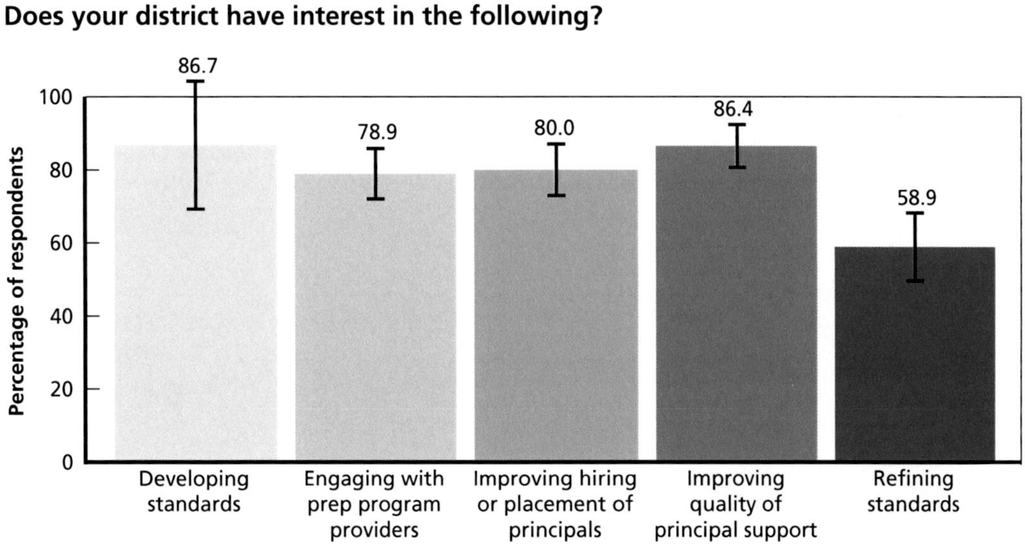

NOTE: Bars reflect weighted survey data from 10K+ district respondents indicating the percentage of districts that indicated moderate or strong interest in developing each pipeline activity. Number of responses varied by question. Districts that did not have standards were asked about their interest in developing them. Districts with standards were asked about their interest in refining them. Error bars represent 95-percent confidence intervals.

communicated at least moderate or strong interest in doing more related to engagement with external principal preparation providers, improving their hiring processes, and improving the quality of support principals received. Similarly, 87 percent of those without leader standards reported a moderate or strong interest in developing standards. Among those with leader standards, just under 60 percent indicated an interest in further refining their standards. We did not observe significant differences based on district size in terms of respondents' interest in improving these areas of their pipeline.

The most commonly cited barriers that district respondents said were preventing them from doing more to improve any area of their principal pipelines were lack of time and funding (Table 2.6). Time particularly appeared to be a factor stymieing the ability to do more to enhance principal evaluation and support, with 54 percent of respondents bringing up lack of time as a barrier (see Table 42 in the supplemental material). Thirty-seven percent of respondents specified lack of time as a barrier to engaging with preservice programs (see Table 37 in the supplemental material). In other pipeline areas (developing or refining standards, improving hiring), about 20–30 percent of respondents also brought up time as an obstacle to improvement. Lack of funding was cited by about one-quarter of respondents as a barrier to improving hiring and engaging with preservice providers, although it came up as a barrier to

Table 2.6
Percentage of 10K+ Districts Reporting Particular Barriers to Improving Pipeline Activities

Barrier	Refining Standards	Developing Standards	Engage with External Partners	Improve Principal Hiring and Placement	Enhance Principal Evaluation and Support
No perceived need	34%	42%	17%	27%	9%
Not enough expertise	2%	0%	1%	6%	1%
Not enough funding/money	6%	0%	22%	21%	40%
Not enough staff	2%	0%	5%	11%	8%
Not enough time	23%	24%	37%	28%	54%
Lack of provider programs in area	–	–	4%	–	–
Lack of provider willingness to collaborate	–	–	19%	–	–
Lack of adequate technology	–	–	–	2%	–
No expressed need among principals	–	–	–	–	0%
Lack of support from stakeholders	–	–	–	–	1%

NOTE: Table created using weighted qualitative code data from respondents in 10K+ districts. Each column represents a separate item asked to respondents with the number of respondents differing by column (see Appendix B for more details).

improving principal support among 40 percent of respondents. Lack of staff or lack of expertise among staff came up much less as a barrier to pipeline improvement across the board (mentioned by only 10 percent or fewer of our respondents).

When asked about factors that would keep them from making pipeline improvements, district officials sometimes said that they did not perceive a need to make improvements at this time. Specifically, between one-quarter and one-third of district respondents indicated no perceived need to develop or refine leader standards or improve hiring. In the area of leader standards, it may be that district leaders felt that their existing state standards were adequate, and thus there was no need to improve upon them. According to our qualitative coding, about 14 percent of respondents said that state guidelines or union contracts kept them from doing more to refine their district standards. As one interviewee explained, "the biggest factor is trying to make sure that we stay within state level guidelines and standards. We don't want to deviate too much from that and cause confusion."

Generally, those with more interest in improving aspects of their pipelines were more apt to note time as a barrier to doing so. For example, of those with a moderate or strong interest in improving hiring and placement, 31 percent cited time as a barrier to doing more, whereas just 6 percent of those with no or slight interest brought up the time barrier. As might be expected, more of those who indicated none or only slight interest in improving particular activities also were likely to cite no perceived need for that improvement.

Broadly, the prevalence of the barriers to developing pipelines we report in Table 2.6 appeared similar across medium and large districts, although we did observe significant differences between these categories for some barriers. For example, about 29 percent of medium districts stated no perceived need to improve their hiring and placement, compared with just 10 percent of those in large districts (see Table 39 in the supplemental material). On the other hand, large districts were more likely than medium districts to note lack of staff or lack of funding as factors that prevented improvement of hiring and placement. In addition, large districts were more likely than medium districts to cite lack of staff or lack of expertise as barriers to improving evaluation and support of school principals (see Table 42 in the supplemental material).

Small Districts Results

Our data-collection strategy was designed to provide a nationally representative sample of responses from 10K+ districts. Nevertheless, we were interested in gathering some responses from small districts—which altogether serve more than 21 million students, or about 45 percent of the nation's public school population—to consider whether the concept of principal pipelines is relevant to these districts. As noted earlier in this report, the evidence about the effect of pipeline activities is based on the experiences of very large school districts that participated in the PPI. To be sure, small districts serving fewer than 10,000 students employ principals and are very likely to engage in at least some pipeline activities. But because they operate far fewer schools and employ fewer principals than larger districts, they may be less likely than larger districts to have central office infrastructure and systems in place. This raises legitimate questions about whether and how pipeline activities would be used by smaller districts. To begin exploring this issue, we reached out to a tiny fraction of small districts (164 out of 12,096 or 1.4 percent). The response rate from these small districts was substantially lower than for the 10K+ districts—10 percent versus 26 percent.

Although the lower response rate in small districts might suggest that officials in those districts are less interested in pipeline activities than those in larger districts, responses from those we did interview from our exploratory group of small districts were similar to those from medium and large districts in many respects. All small district respondents reported that their district's goals, strategic plans, or initiatives tied school leadership to school improvement, compared with the vast majority of medium and large districts. As with medium and large districts, about half of the respondents in small districts reported moderate or high satisfaction with their pool. The most common gaps in the available pool of candidates to fill principal vacancies described by respondents in small districts were similar to those described in medium and large

Figure 2.7
Percentage of Small Districts Noting Presence of Particular Principal Pipeline Activities

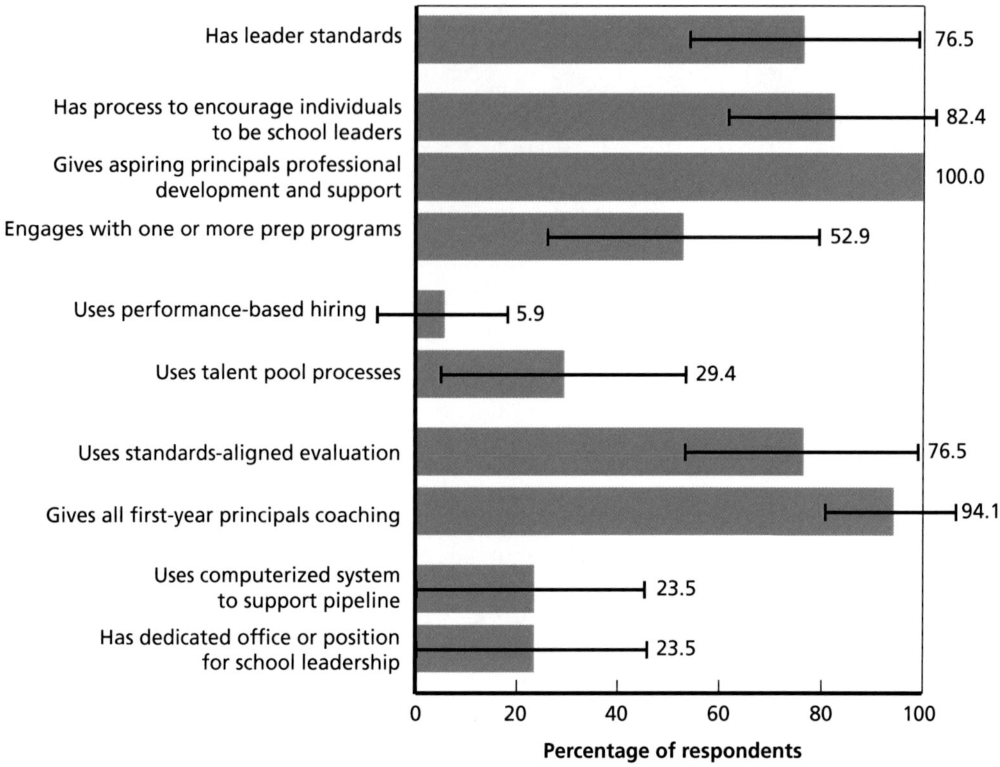

NOTE: Bars reflect weighted survey data from respondents in small districts (n = 17). Error bars represent 95-percent confidence intervals.

districts, although fewer in small districts indicated a gap in candidates from specific ethnic groups (13 percent).

Figure 2.7 summarizes the reported prevalence of ten pipeline activities in the small districts that participated in our interviews. A clear majority of respondents reported that their small district had leader standards, provided support and encouragement for aspiring principals, and used standards-based principal evaluation.

We were somewhat surprised to see that 53 percent of respondents from small districts reported engaging with one or more preservice program. Furthermore, of those who responded that they engage with one or more preservice program, 69 percent reported that they hired at least one candidate from a program with which they engage, and 44 percent reported hiring at least half of their principals from a program with which they have engagement (see Tables 17–18 in the supplemental material).

Because the development of such systems as leader tracking and talent pools can involve fixed costs that might be more difficult for smaller districts to absorb (see

Kaufman et al., 2017), we anticipated that respondents from smaller districts would be less likely to report having and using such systems. As predicted, only 24 percent of those in small districts indicated having a computerized data system or a position or office dedicated to school leadership, and 29 percent reported that they have a talent pool. All small district respondents reported engaging in at least two pipeline activities, with 65 percent of respondents stating that they engaged in five of ten pipeline activities.

When it came to hiring processes, the most common criteria small district leaders reported using to evaluate principal candidates were responses to interview questions (47 percent), feedback from community or other stakeholder groups (41 percent), leader standards (29 percent), and teaching or leadership experience (29 percent). Only 6 percent of small district respondents reported using performance tasks (see Table 38 in the supplemental material).

With regard to principal supervision, 71 percent of respondents from small districts reported that the superintendent was the only supervisor of principals in the district. This contrasts with 12 percent for 10K+ districts. The reported average number of principals supervised by one supervisor in small districts was just fewer than five but ranged from one to 20 (see Table 45 in the supplemental material). Eighty-two percent of small district respondents reported that the principal supervisor was also providing coaching and mentoring for principals (see Table 40 in the supplemental material).

Small district responses about coaching and mentoring suggest potential differences with 10K+ districts (see Tables 40 and 41 in the supplemental material). Seventy-five percent of small district respondents reported that their district provides funding to support principals to pursue training or further education on their own outside of the district. In contrast, 37 percent of respondents from 10K+ districts reported supporting principals this way. Forty-seven percent of small district respondents reported that coaching and mentoring were provided by an organization or person from outside the district, while 22 percent of respondents from 10K+ districts reported such involvement from outside the district. Very few small district respondents reported that their district provided training for principals (12 percent) or supported principal professional learning communities (6 percent). Among 10K+ district respondents, 49 percent reported that their district provided training for principals and 40 percent said their district provided principal professional learning communities. As noted in Figure 2.8, most of the officials in small districts who participated in our study expressed interest in improving their pipeline activities.

Figure 2.8
Percentage of Small Districts Reporting Moderate or Strong Interest in Developing Pipeline Activities

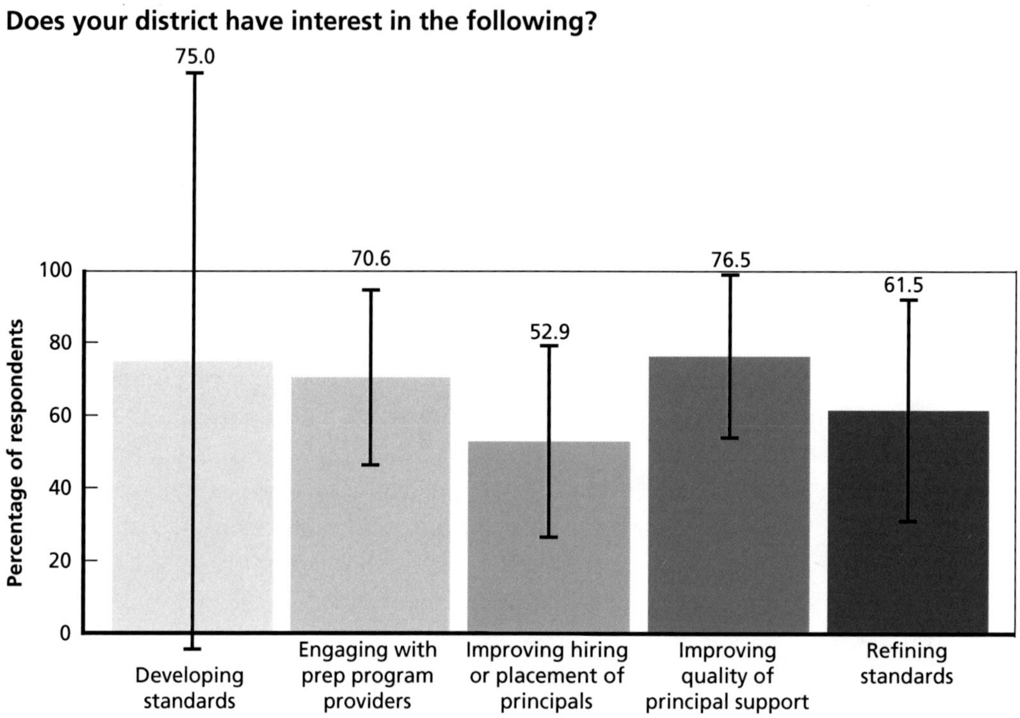

NOTE: Bars reflect weighted survey data from respondents in small districts (*n* = 17). Districts without standards were asked about their interest in developing them. Districts with standards were asked about their interest in refining them. Error bars represent 95-percent confidence intervals.

CHAPTER THREE

Discussion and Conclusions

This report provides an initial snapshot of how much U.S. school districts are focused on developing and improving pipelines for preparing, hiring, and supporting school principals. Findings from a comprehensive evaluation of the PPI (Gates et al., 2019) linked principal pipelines to increased achievement and retention of the principal workforce, underscoring the need for more information about the prevalence of pipeline activities and the potential opportunities for states and districts to support improvements to principal pipelines.

Findings from this study—derived from interviews with officials from 10K+ districts—indicate that a vast majority (90 percent) of these districts regard school leadership as a key aspect of school improvement, yet a majority see room for improvement in their principal candidates. Responses also suggest that most districts are familiar with and engaged in pipeline activities. All districts were able to identify an individual or group responsible for principal supervision. Of the ten principal pipeline activities that we focused our interviews on, respondents from all school districts reported engaging in at least two, nearly all reported engaging in at least three, and three-quarters of districts reported engaging in five pipeline activities. Only about 1 percent of 10K+ districts indicated engaging in all of the pipeline activities we explicitly asked about; however, this should not be interpreted as a deficit. The vision of strategic pipelines outlined in the PPI was not that all pipeline activities would be comprehensively embraced but that they would be prioritized and tailored to the district context (Turnbull et al., 2016).

Three-quarters or more of the 10K+ district respondents communicated at least moderate or strong interest in doing more related to engagement with external principal preparation providers, improving their hiring processes, and improving the quality of support that principals received. Among those respondents who did not yet have leader standards, 87 percent reported a moderate or strong interest in developing them. Those with leaders' standards were somewhat less likely to express interest in refining them.

We also saw some associations between reported engagement in certain pipeline activities and reported satisfaction with the principal candidate pool. In particular, when districts reported giving aspiring principals professional development support, engaging with at least one preparation program, standards-aligned evaluation, or giving all first-year principals coaching, they were more likely to report satisfaction with their candidate pool. These associations do not imply that the pipeline activities caused greater satisfaction but point to areas where more systematic research could yield useful insights about the implications of pipeline activities.

We found that respondents from large districts were more likely than respondents from medium districts to report having

- school leadership standards
- processes to encourage individuals to become school leaders
- standards-aligned evaluation
- objective criteria, such as performance tasks to evaluate principal candidates
- a dedicated office of school leadership.

The number of principal pipeline activities in which districts report engaging may not be as consequential for improving school leadership as the depth and quality with which districts engage in various pipeline activities. Leader standards were a key emphasis of the PPI, and all six PPI districts created or refined their leader standards as part of the initiative and then used them as a basis to inform other pipeline activities. Responses from our national sample suggest that kind of continual focus on leader standards may not be happening as much in most U.S. school districts. Thirty percent of 10K+ districts cited relying solely on state leader standards and not any district-specific standards, which suggests that they may not be reflecting on how state standards could be tailored and applied to emphasize and support district priorities. Furthermore, about 40 percent of those districts with leader standards indicated little to no interest in refining them.

Nearly half of district officials reported a lack of diversity among principal candidates, although the respondents did not report actively engaging in strategies to attract more diverse candidates. Some respondents specified that schools lacked both a diverse principal workforce and a diverse teacher pool from which to draw; this was mentioned by district leaders in conjunction with a statement about shifting student demographics.

Hiring processes appeared to vary widely across districts, with districts describing a range of criteria they look for and methods they use to gather information about candidates. Just more than half of 10K+ district officials reported that their district uses a talent pool process, and less 20 percent mentioned performance-based tasks when describing their hiring processes. Instead, interviews were by far the most commonly reported method for evaluating principal candidates.

Interview responses suggest that principal supervision and on-the-job support, in particular, may vary dramatically across districts in terms of who provides the supervision and support, the forms that support takes, and the intensity of that supervision and support. Leaders from the 10K+ district sample reported that principal supervisors were overseeing anywhere from three to 40 principals, as well as variation in terms of whether the person evaluating the principal is also providing the support.

Potential Policy Implications

Our research suggests that many districts—particularly medium-sized districts serving 10,000–49,999 students—might benefit from some guidance and tools that would support strengthening their principal pipelines, given the strong interest among most districts for this. In particular, our findings suggest that all districts could benefit from more ways to develop and communicate about their leader standards. Medium districts specifically could benefit from supports to help them collaborate productively with preservice providers and develop improved methods and criteria for evaluating principal candidates that build on state evaluation rubrics; evaluation tools, such as the Vanderbilt Assessment of Leadership in Education (Vanderbilt Assessment of Leadership in Education, undated); or competency assessments used by PPI districts or preservice providers.

Eighty percent of respondents expressed interest in improving their hiring processes. However, districts in our sample reported a wide range of methods and criteria to hire principals. At the same time, evidence about what practices are most effective is lacking. To support districts in hiring, organizations and entities supporting principals might consider developing repositories of school leader performance tasks or other assessments that can be accessed for free or at low cost. Better and more assessments of interpersonal skills and leadership styles might be especially welcome, given that so many of our interviewees cited such interpersonal characteristics as a particular area of focus in evaluating principal candidates.

Districts would also likely welcome more guidance and strategies for identifying and improving their pool of principal candidates of diverse ethnicities. About half of those with whom we spoke acknowledged the lack of principals of diverse ethnicities as a gap but also did not say much about strategies they were using to improve the diversity of their principal workforce. Some respondents specifically reported a lack of diversity in the teachers and candidate pool from which principals might come. The lack of diversity among public school teachers has been well documented (U.S. Department of Education, 2016). Thus, efforts to enhance the diversity of principal candidates may need to reach back to include or at least coordinate with programs designed to enhance the diversity of the teacher workforce (Stevens and Motamedi, 2019).

On-the-job support and evaluation for principals is an area that districts have reported already emphasizing but also see as in need of improvement. This suggests that districts may benefit from more information and options for principal support and evaluation. There is evidence of success for a few specific leadership development programs (see Herman et al., 2017), but more research is needed about effective evaluation and support practices (Davis et al., 2011; Shelton, 2013). Research and feedback from the education field could improve understanding about the right number of principals that should be supervised by one person, factors influencing that optimal span of control, and the most productive role for supervisors in terms of the coaching they offer (and whether coaching should be provided by a separate person or group). Similarly, more research might provide better information about the types of professional development and support that are most useful to principals and how that varies by context.

Given that respondents from large districts reported more experience with pipeline activities compared with those from medium and small districts, large districts might be tapped to provide guidance and support to medium and small districts. Through deeper networks and engagement opportunities, those large districts could potentially mentor smaller districts and even create such mechanisms as residencies and other tools in partnership with them. Preparation programs and the state entities that oversee them might think about ways to engage with smaller districts. Ongoing efforts from the University Principal Pipeline Initiative might yield useful examples of such collaborations in preparation programs among districts (Wang et al., 2018).

Finally, responses from our exploratory sample of small districts suggest that principal supervision may be structured very differently in these districts compared with supervision in 10K+ districts. Notably, respondents in small districts were far more likely than respondents in 10K+ districts to report that superintendents directly supervise principals and that districts rely on outside organizations or individuals to provide coaching. Respondents in small districts were less likely to report that their districts provide support through professional learning communities and other forms of support. At the same time, the similarities we observed among engagement in some pipeline activities in small districts versus 10K+ districts imply that those districts might also benefit from more support for pipeline activities, possibly through more networks and consortiums of small districts. Regardless, our findings in small districts suggest that more research across a more comprehensive sample of those districts about their requirements related to school leadership is needed and caution should be taken when applying insights from the PPI to the smallest districts in the United States.

APPENDIX A

Data Collection

The National Pipeline Baseline Survey aims to gather baseline information about the prevalence of pipeline activities in districts across the country. We sought to describe the current state of development of principal pipelines across the United States, overall and then separately by district size category. We grouped districts into five size categories as described in Table A.1. For reporting and discussion purposes, we condensed these five categories into three groups: large, medium, and small.

Sample Design

The sampling strategy was designed to generate a nationally representative estimate that shows the extent to which districts around the country are engaged and interested in pipeline activities while enabling comparisons between estimates for different district size categories. There are more than 13,000 school districts in the country, and the size distribution is extremely skewed, with more than 12,000 districts serving fewer than 10,000 students. To effectively balance competing aims of capturing responses from larger school districts most likely to engage in pipeline activities while also gathering responses from smaller districts to understand the extent to which these activities are interesting and relevant to them, our sample included all districts serving more than 20,000 students and randomly stratified samples of smaller districts (0–9,999 students and 10,000–19,999 students).

We constructed a sampling frame using a list purchased from MDR in September 2019, which included individual and institution information for all public U.S. K–12 school districts. We narrowed the sampling frame by removing charter school local education agencies (LEAs), supervisory unions (i.e., collections of smaller districts),[1] Department of Defense Education Activity LEAs, "subdistrict" observations (e.g., Chicago Public School District Zone 1), and observations not identified as

[1] Supervisory unions are administrative, planning, and educational service units made up of two or more school districts. About 300 school districts in the sampling frame are identified by National Center for Education Statistics (NCES) as belonging to a supervisory union, with the vast majority of unions being located in New Hamp-

"[r]egular public school districts" by the 2018–2019 NCES Common Core Data. Those restrictions yielded a final sampling frame of 13,012 U.S. public school districts. From this frame, we placed the districts into five size categories based on student enrollment, as reported in the MDR data.

Concurrent with the interview effort, The Wallace Foundation was supporting TA on principal pipelines for school districts around the country. All districts serving 50,000 or more students were invited to participate in the TA, and about half chose to do so. The Foundation also invited some medium districts to participate in the TA effort. Our study *included* all large districts in the country, regardless of whether they chose to participate in the TA.[2] At the request of The Wallace Foundation, we *excluded* from our study medium districts that chose to participate in the TA out of concern about the potential burden participation might pose for these smaller districts. Compared with other districts in their same enrollment category, TA-participating districts were more likely to be classified by NCES as a "city" school district and serve larger percentages of nonwhite and FRPL-eligible students.

After implementing these exclusions, we randomly selected districts in the moderate and small categories to participate in the study. Table A.1 provides information about the total number of districts, TA participation, contacts, and completed interviews by size category.

Table A.1
Sample Description

Category	Student Enrollment	Total Student Enrollment for Category (millions)	Total Number of Districts Nationwide	Number of Districts Participating in Wallace TA	Number of Districts Contacted for Interview	Number of Interviews Completed
5 (large)	99,000+	6.9	30	16	30	16 (9)[a]
4 (large)	50,000–98,999	4.5	68	34	68	29 (20)[a]
3 (medium)	20,000–49,999	8.0	301	33	268	73
2 (medium)	10,000–19,999	7.0	520	2	300	57
1 (small)	0–9,999	21.4	12,096	0	164	17

SOURCE: RAND calculations based on data about U.S. public K–12 school districts provided by MDR and information on TA participation provided by The Wallace Foundation in September 2019.
[a] Number in parentheses represents the number of completed interviews with districts participating in TA.

shire and Vermont. If districts included in the sample belong to a supervisory union, the survey team will be made aware of this fact and inquire whether district or supervisory union leadership is most appropriate to interview.

2 We also included districts in these categories that had participated in a Wallace Foundation initiative (e.g., PPI, Principal Supervisors Initiative, University Principal Preparation Initiative).

Recruitment and Data Collection

We began contacting districts on October 16, 2019, and completed a total of 192 interviews by December 20, 2019. During the course of data collection, we contacted 830 school districts. We reached out to all districts serving 20,000 students or more after implementing exclusions already described. We also reached out to 300 districts serving between 10,000 and 19,999 students and another 164 districts serving fewer than 10,000 students. These districts were randomly selected after implementing exclusions already described.

The recruitment approach consisted of mailing (via FedEx or first-class mail, depending on address availability) a recruitment letter to the selected school district to invite a senior staff to participate in the study. The recruitment letter provided background information about the study, the goal of the study, and contact information. A few days after the mailing, an initial phone call was made to identify the senior district staff to participate in the phone interview. We recontacted nonrespondents up to eight times to request their participation in an interview. In subsequent recruitment waves, we opted for email rather than mail recruitment letters, given that email appeared to be the preferred and more effective mode of communication with district-level personnel. We sent one recruitment email and up to three follow up emails to nonrespondents. Once we identified the respondent and scheduled a phone interview, a confirmation email and a calendar invite was sent to the respondent. The day prior to the interview, a reminder email or call was made to the respondent.

Our staffing structure consisted of a team of ten data collectors from the RAND Survey Research Group (SRG) and RAND Labor and Education division. All data collectors conducted phone interviews; five data collectors were lead recruiters. The lead recruiter's role was to make the initial phone outreach to school district staff and schedule a 20–30-minute phone interview with the superintendent, assistant superintendent, or another senior staff. The lead recruiters scheduled interviews either for themselves or for phone interviewers based on staff availability. The average time per interview was 30 minutes, with interview length ranging from 15 to 57 minutes.

The data-collection team participated in a three-day training following SRG standard phone interviewer procedures. They covered were overall project goals, study protocol, phone interviewer principles, qualitative and quantitative data capture, qualitative coding principles, and functionality of the case management platform. At the end of the training, interviewers became certified by successfully passing a mock interview exercise. The lead recruiters had additional trainings on outreach procedures, recruitment guidelines, and use of the scheduling system platform.

We held regular recruitment meetings with lead recruiters to further refine recruitment strategies and customize outreach based on school district enrollment size. The project director monitored 10 percent of interviews to ensure interviewers' adherence to protocol and accuracy in data capture. In addition, the project director oversaw day-to-day data-collection activities and monitored interviewer productivity, data quality, and response rates.

We also held weekly team meetings with all interviewers to ensure qualitative coding reliability and to identify any issues encountered with interviews. We discuss the details of our qualitative coding process in Appendix B.

Completed Interviews

Our overall response rate was 23 percent—or 192 out of 830 districts contacted for this study. Nonrespondents included hard refusals (13 percent), nonresponse or inability to complete the interview within the short data-collection window (63 percent), and districts that would not allow us to conduct an interview without completing a district research approval process (1 percent). Two small districts were deemed ineligible because the district did not hire principals. The response rate varied by district size category. Among large districts (categories 4 and 5), our overall response rate was 46 percent, but it was only 26 percent among category 4 districts serving between 50,000 and 98,999 students who did not participate in the TA. The latter was similar to the response rate among medium districts (23 percent)—none of which participated in TA. The response rate for small districts was substantially lower, at 10 percent.

Interviewees predominantly served in districts classified as "city" or "suburban" by NCES, with the average responding district consisting of about 60 percent nonwhite students and 50 percent students being FRPL-eligible (see Table B.1 for additional detail on sample characteristics). Among the 192 districts that responded, 29 were participating in The Wallace Foundation's TA efforts; all were large districts in categories 4 and 5.

In 15 cases, we spoke with more than one person during a single district interview for a total of 217 interviews in 192 districts. When reporting findings, we counted each district interview as a single response regardless of the number of individuals involved in this interview.

Our interviewees included 55 superintendents; 88 associate, assistant, or area superintendents (seven with *leadership* in their title and 15 with *human resources, human capital,* or *talent* in their title); and 74 leaders with other titles, such as executive director, chief, or director (19 with *leadership* in their title and 27 with *human resources, human capital,* or *talent* in their title).

Development of Interview Protocol

The interview protocol was designed to gather information about the topics of interest in an efficient and systematic manner. The interview protocol covered the following topic areas:

- extent to which their district views school principals as a key lever for school improvement
- extent to which they are satisfied with their current pool of candidates for principal vacancies
- whether their district is engaged in specific pipeline activities to prepare, hire, support, and retain principals
- level of interest in specific pipeline activities and perceived barriers to implementing them.

We used prior data-collection instruments (surveys, interviews, and focus groups) from the evaluation of the principal pipeline initiative as a starting point (Gates et al., 2019). We also leveraged a rubric developed by Policy Studies Associates to use in the TA effort organized by The Wallace Foundation to support districts in implementing comprehensive principal pipelines during school year 2019–2020 (Policy Studies Associates, forthcoming).

At the time we were designing the instrument, we were considering two possible options for gathering data from sampled districts that were participating in the TA: Conduct interviews with district representatives as we would with non-TA districts or develop a mechanism to extract data from the TA process. Although we ultimately decided against extracting data from the TA process, we developed our instrument to align with language used in the TA rubric. Future studies may be able to take advantage of this alignment to combine different data sources.

In developing the questions, we made a conscious effort to limit the use of jargon from the PPI. As our goal was to design a set of questions that could be broadly understood by any district official and could be completed in 20–30 minutes. We intentionally prioritized closed-ended questions combined with a limited number of open-ended questions on carefully selected topics.

We obtained feedback on the draft instrument from Brenda Turnbull of Policy Studies Associates and Ty Wilde and Bronwyn Bevan at The Wallace Foundation. We also obtained input on the instrument from four individuals (Jevelyn Bonner-Reed, Mikel Royal, Douglas Anthony, and Glenn Pethel) who were district officials in PPI districts during the initiative.

APPENDIX B

Data Analysis

The data collection yielded a total of 192 valid district responses. Because we undersampled category 1 (small) districts and our response rate for that category was low, we opted to focus our analysis on weighting and summarizing closed-ended interview responses in categories 2–5 that served 10,000 or more students (10K+ districts). Responses from small districts are left unweighted and considered exploratory. In the next section, we describe our survey-weighting procedures for the 10K+ districts and provide additional detail for analytic methods used in the main report.

Survey Weighting

We estimated survey weights for each of the 175 respondents from 10K+ districts such that these districts reflect the characteristics of the 10+K districts nationally. These weights were calculated using the combination of three separate weighting procedures.

First, we calculated sample selection weights for each respondent. These weights are defined as the inverse probability of selection into the sample. Because we stratify our sample along five district size categories (see Table B.1), the probability of selection is defined as $1/N_{CAT}$, where N_{CAT} is the population total of districts in that size category.

Second, we estimated survey response weights for each respondent, which is the inverse of the estimated probability that a sampled district would respond to the interview. We estimated these probabilities separately for each size category using a logistic regression model that models a binary indicator of survey response as a function of a district's (1) total student enrollment; (2) proportion student race and ethnicity enrollment (percentage of white, black, Native American, Hispanic), LEP enrollment, and FRPL enrollment; (3) binary indicators for whether a district contains any schools on their state's "focus" or "priority" lists; and (4) binary indicators for school urbanicity (city, suburb, town, rural) as defined by NCES. We used these models to estimate the predicted probabilities of survey response for each respondent. To avoid extreme survey response weights, rather than use the raw predicted response probabilities to form weights, we instead divided respondents into quartiles based on their predicted response probabilities and calculate the mean predicted response probability within that quartile. We took the inverse of these mean predicted response probabilities to form the survey response weight for each respondent.

Finally, we performed an iterative raking procedure to improve the extent to which the characteristics of our 10K+ sample match the characteristics of 10K+ districts in the population. Specifically, the raking procedure takes the product of the sample selection and survey response weights as a "base weight" and calibrates this weight such that the weighted sample matches the population totals of the following demographic categories:

- district size category (2–5)
- percentage of white student enrollment (0–24, 25–49, 50–74, 75–100)
- percentage of black student enrollment (0–24, 25–49, 50–74, 75–100)
- percentage of Hispanic student enrollment (0–24, 25–49, 50–74, 75–100)
- percentage of FRPL-eligible enrollment (0–24, 25–49, 50–74, 75–100).

Although we have additional demographic variables that could be added to the calibration process, because of the number of 10K+ respondents (n = 175), the inclusion of additional calibration variables led to inconsistent convergence of the raking model. We use the calibrated weights that resulted from this raking procedure as the weights used in the final analysis to estimate results for this report. For all results, we use Taylor series linearization to provide estimates of variation for survey weighted results.

Sample Representativeness

In Table B.1 we present descriptive statistics for the (1) unweighted 10K+ sample, (2) weighted 10K+ sample, and (3) 10K+ population. As evidenced by the unweighted 10K+ sample characteristics, prior to weighting, the 10K+ sample and population appear reasonably similar, with the largest differences being in total district enrollment (i.e., district size), percentage of white enrollment, and district urbanicity. After applying survey weights, the sample and population means align more closely, with the largest discrepancies being in the percentage of suburban and city districts, where the sample and population values differ by 2 and 3 percentage points, respectively. In all cases, the 95-percent confidence intervals from the weighted sample bracket the population means on all characteristics presented in Table B.1.

Qualitative Analysis

The interview protocol contained 17 open-ended questions to gather richer information from district respondents about the nature of their pipeline challenges,

Table B.1
Percentage of 10K+ District Characteristics (Unweighted, Weighted, Population)

	Unweighted 10K+ Sample			Weighted 10K+ Sample			10K+ Population		
District Characteristics	Mean	Low 95%	Hi 95%	Mean	Low 95%	Hi 95%	Mean	Low 95% CI	Hi 95% CI
White enrollment	40	37	44	45	40	50	44	43	46
Black enrollment	17	14	19	16	13	18	16	15	17
Native American enrollment	1	0	1	1	0	1	1	0	1
Asian enrollment	6	5	7	6	4	8	7	6	7
Hispanic enrollment	36	32	40	32	27	37	32	30	34
LEP enrollment	13	11	14	11	9	13	11	11	12
FRPL enrollment	55	51	58	53	48	57	52	50	54
Has one or more focus school	43	36	51	39	31	47	39	35	42
Has one or more priority school	28	21	35	26	19	33	25	22	28
Rural district	3	1	6	8	2	13	7	6	9
Town district	3	1	6	4	1	7	2	1	3
Suburban district	51	44	59	50	41	58	48	45	51
City district	42	34	49	39	31	47	42	39	46
District size 2	33	26	40	57	54	60	56	53	60
District size 3	42	34	49	33	30	36	34	30	37
District size 4	17	11	22	7	6	9	7	5	9
District size 5	9	5	13	3	3	4	3	2	4

SOURCE: RAND calculations based on data about U.S. public K–12 school districts provided by MDR in September 2019.

what these pipeline activities look like on the ground, and what barriers they perceive to implementing these activities. The full interview instrument is available at the end of this appendix.

Open-ended questions were categorized using predefined codes reflecting expected themes in responses, based on research team experience in studying principal pipelines. We refined these codes in the first several weeks of interviews based on topics discussed in the interviews. All coding was done by those conducting the interviews, although double coding was conducted by two master coders (researchers deeply familiar with principal pipelines). These master coders double coded 11 percent of the interviews along with interviewers over a period of several weeks. For any disagreements between one master coder and interviewer, the two master coders came to consensus on the best code.

We discussed any substantial disagreements in the coding, as well as any necessary updates to the coding plan, at weekly meetings with all interviewers. During the first and second week of coding, inter-rater reliability was 64 percent and 61 percent, respectively.[1] By the third week, inter-rater reliability between the master coders and interviewers was 82 percent. Given low inter-rater reliability on interviews coded in the first few weeks, one master coder reviewed all 20 interviews coded before the third week and made decisions on final codes for those interviews.

Regression Analysis

For 10K+ districts, we estimate that respondents' self-reported use of any particular pipeline activity was associated with the probability that they indicated that they were "satisfied" or "very satisfied" with the pool of candidates available to fill principal vacancies. To do so, we fit ten separate linear probability models,[2] one for each pipeline activity, that regressed a binary indicator set to 1 if a respondent indicated they were "satisfied" or "very satisfied" with their pool of candidates on a binary indicator for whether a respondent indicated doing that particular pipeline activity in their district, alongside controls for district urbanicity; total enrollment; district percentage of white, black, Native American, Hispanic, Asian, and Indian students; district percentage of LEP and FRPL-eligible students; whether the district had at least one school on their state's "focus" or "priority" list; and their district size category. These regression models were weighted with the survey weights used to produce the descriptive statistics. In Table B.2, we list the point estimates, standard errors, and statistical significance for each of the ten pipeline activities.

---

1 Inter-rater reliability was calculated as the total number of coded open-ended responses coded the same way by the master coder and interviewer divided by the total number of coded open-ended responses.

2 As respondents in all districts were able to identify the person responsible for principal's supervision (Principal Pipeline Activity #9), there was no variation in prevalence of that activity. It was not included in the regression analysis.

Table B.2
Pipeline Activity Estimates for Pipeline Satisfaction Analysis

Pipeline Activity	β	Standard Error	Statistical Significance
District has leader standards	0.17	0.11	
District has process to encourage individuals to be school leaders	0.22	0.15	
District gives aspiring principals PD and support	0.35	0.14	**
District engages with at least one preparation program	0.18	0.09	*
District uses talent pool	0.001	0.09	
District uses performance-based hiring	0.12	0.10	
District uses standards-aligned evaluation	0.25	0.09	***
District gives all first-year principals individual coaching	0.31	0.13	**
District uses computerized system to support principal pipeline	0.07	0.09	
District has dedicated office or position for school leadership	0.10	0.08	

NOTE: * $p < 0.05$, ** $p < 0.01$ *** $p < 0.001$. Table presents the estimated change in probability of 10K+ respondent (n = 175) satisfaction with principal candidate pool associated with having or engaging in each of the ten principal pipeline activities. Each row represents a separate linear probability model in which a binary indicator of satisfaction is regressed on an indicator for whether the respondent indicated having or engaging with that activity and a vector of district characteristics.

References

Acharya, Ashwin, Roni Lieber, Lissa Seem, and Tom Welchman, "How to Identify the Right 'Spans of Control' for Your Organization," McKinsey & Company webpage, December 21, 2017. As of May 11, 2020:
https://www.mckinsey.com/business-functions/organization/our-insights/how-to-identify-the-right-spans-of-control-for-your-organization

Aguilar, Elena, Davina Goldwasser, and Kristina Tank-Crestetto, "Support Transform, Principals Schools," *Educational Leadership*, Vol. 69, No. 2, October 2011, pp. 70–73. As of May 14, 2020:
http://www.ascd.org/publications/educational-leadership/oct11/vol69/num02/Support-Principals,-Transform-Schools.aspx

Anderson, Leslie M., and Brenda J. Turnbull, *Sustaining a Principal Pipeline*, Washington, D.C.: Policy Studies Associates, Inc., February 2019. As of May 14, 2020:
https://www.wallacefoundation.org/knowledge-center/pages/sustainability-of-principal-pipeline-initiative.aspx

Anderson, Leslie M., Brenda J. Turnbull, and Erikson R. Arcaira, *Leader Tracking Systems: Turning Data into Information for School Leadership*, Washington, D.C.: Policy Studies Associates, Inc., June 2017. As of May 14, 2020:
https://www.wallacefoundation.org/knowledge-center/Documents/Leader-Tracking-Systems-Turning-Data-Into-Information-for-School-Leadership.pdf

Béteille, Tara, Demetra Kalogrides, and Susanna Loeb, "Stepping Stones: Principal Career Paths and School Outcomes," *Social Science Research*, Vol. 41, No. 4, 2012, pp. 904–919. As of May 14, 2020:
https://doi.org/10.1016/j.ssresearch.2012.03.003

Bowers, Alex J., and Bradford R. White, "Do Principal Preparation and Teacher Qualifications Influence Different Types of School Growth Trajectories in Illinois? A Growth Mixture Model Analysis," *Journal of Educational Administration*, Vol. 52, No. 5, July 2014, pp. 705–736. As of May 14, 2020:
https://doi.org/10.1108/JEA-12-2012-0134

Briggs, Kerri L., Gretchen Rhines Cheney, Jacquelyn Davis, and Kerry Ann Moll, *Operating in the Dark: What Outdated State Policies and Data Gaps Mean for Effective School Leadership*, Dallas, Tex.: George W. Bush Institute, July 29, 2013. As of May 14, 2020:
https://www.bushcenter.org/publications/resources-reports/reports/operating-in-the-dark-what-outdated-state-policies-and-data-gaps-mean-for-effective-school-leadership.html

Clifford, Matthew, *Hiring Quality School Leaders: Challenges and Emerging Practices*, Washington, D.C.: American Institutes for Research, February 1, 2010. As of May 14, 2020:
https://www.air.org/resource/hiring-quality-school-leaders-challenges-and-emerging-practices

Copeland, Glenda, and Ann Neeley, *Identifying Competencies and Actions of Effective Turnaround Principals*, Metairie, La.: Southeast Comprehensive Center, briefing paper, January 2013. As of May 14, 2020:
http://www.sedl.org/secc/resources/briefs/effective_turnaround_principals/

Corcoran, Amanda, Michael Casserly, Ricki Price-Baugh, Denise Walston, Robin Hall, and Candace Simon, *Rethinking Leadership: The Changing Role of Principal Supervisors*, Washington, D.C.: Council of Great City Schools, October 2013. As of May 14, 2020:
https://www.wallacefoundation.org/knowledge-center/Documents/Rethinking-Leadership-The-Changing-Role-of-Principal-Supervisors.pdf

Danielson Group, "A Vision of Excellence," webpage, undated. As of May 15, 2020:
http://www.danielsongroup.org/framework/

Darling-Hammond, Linda, Michelle LaPointe, Debra Meyerson, Margaret Terry Orr, and Carol Cohen, *Preparing School Leaders for a Changing World: Lessons from Exemplary Leadership Development Programs*, Stanford, Calif.: Stanford University, Stanford Educational Leadership Institute, School Leadership Study Final Report, 2007. As of May 14, 2020:
http://www.wallacefoundation.org/knowledge-center/school-leadership/key-research/Documents/Preparing-School-Leaders.pdf

Davis, Jacquelyn, *Improving University Principal Preparation Programs: Five Themes from the Field*, New York, N.Y.: The Wallace Foundation, 2016. As of May 14, 2020:
https://www.wallacefoundation.org/knowledge-center/pages/improving-university-principal-preparation-programs.aspx

Davis, Stephen H., Karen Kearney, Nancy M. Sanders, Christopher N. Thomas, and Ronald J. Leon, *The Policies and Practices of Principal Evaluation: A Review of the Literature*, San Francisco, Calif.: WestEd, 2011. As of May 14, 2020:
http://www.wested.org/online_pubs/resource1104.pdf

Gates, Susan M., Matthew D. Baird, Benjamin K. Master, and Emilio R. Chavez-Herrerias, *Principal Pipelines: A Feasible, Affordable, and Effective Way for Districts to Improve Schools*, Santa Monica, Calif.: RAND Corporation, RR-2666-WF, 2019. As of May 14, 2020:
http://www.rand.org/pubs/research_reports/RR2666.html

Gates, Susan, Julia H. Kaufman, Sy Doan, Andrea Prado Tuma., and Deborah Kim, *Taking Stock of Principal Pipelines: What Public School Districts Are Doing and Want to Do to Improve School Leadership—Supplemental Material*, Santa Monica, Calif.: RAND Corporation, RR-A274-2, 2020. As of May 14, 2020:
http://www.rand.org/pubs/research_reports/RRA274-1.html

Goldring, Ellen B., Jason A. Grissom, Mollie Rubin, Laura K. Rogers, Michael Neel, and Melissa Clark, *A New Role Emerges for Principal Supervisors: Evidence from Six Districts in the Principal Supervisor Initiative*, New York, N.Y.: The Wallace Foundation, July 2018. As of May 14, 2020:
https://www.wallacefoundation.org/knowledge-center/pages/a-new-role-emerges-for-principal-supervisors.aspx

Grissom, Jason A., and Susanna Loeb, "Triangulating Principal Effectiveness: How Perspectives of Parents, Teachers, and Assistant Principals Identify the Central Importance of Managerial Skills," *American Educational Research Journal*, Vol. 48, No. 5, October 1, 2011, pp. 1091–1123. As of May 14, 2020:
https://journals.sagepub.com/doi/abs/10.3102/0002831211402663

Grissom, Jason A., Hajime Mitani, and David S. Woo, "Principal Preparation Programs and Principal Outcomes," *Educational Administration Quarterly*, Vol. 55, No. 1, July 2018, pp. 73–115. As of May 14, 2020:
https://journals.sagepub.com/doi/abs/10.1177/0013161X18785865

Guilfoyle, Christy, "Principal Evaluation and Professional Growth," *Policy Priorities*, Vol. 19, No. 2, Summer 2013, pp. 1–3, 5–7. As of May 14, 2020:
http://www.ascd.org/publications/newsletters/policy-priorities/vol19/num02/Principal-Evaluation-and-Professional-Growth.aspx

Harvey, James, and Holly Holland, "The School Principal as Leader: Guiding Schools to Better Teaching and Learning," New York, N.Y.: The Wallace Foundation, January 2013. As of May 14, 2020:
https://www.wallacefoundation.org/knowledge-center/pages/the-school-principal-as-leader-guiding-schools-to-better-teaching-and-learning.aspx

Herman, Rebecca, Susan M. Gates, Aziza Arifkhanova, Mark Barrett, Andriy Bega, Emilio R. Chavez-Herreias, Eugeniu Han, Mark Harris, Katya Migacheva, Rachel Ross, Jennifer T. Leschitz, and Stephani L. Wrabel, *School Leadership Interventions Under the Every Student Succeeds Act: Evidence Review*, Santa Monica, Calif.: RAND Corporation, RR-1550-3-WF, 2017. As of May 14, 2020:
https://www.rand.org/pubs/research_reports/RR1550-3.html

Kaufman, Julia H., Susan M. Gates, Melody Harvey, Yan Wang, and Mark Barrett, *What It Takes to Operate and Maintain Principal Pipelines: Costs and Other Resources*, Santa Monica, Calif.: RAND Corporation, RR-2078-WF, 2017. As of May 14, 2020:
http://www.rand.org/pubs/research_reports/RR2078.html

Leithwood, Kenneth, Karen Seashore Louis, Stephen Anderson, and Kyla Wahlstrom, *Review of Research: How Leadership Influences Student Learning*, New York, N.Y.: The Wallace Foundation, 2004. As of May 14, 2020:
https://www.wallacefoundation.org/knowledge-center/Documents/How-Leadership-Influences-Student-Learning.pdf

Liebowitz, David D., and Lorna Porter, "The Effect of Principal Behaviors on Student, Teacher, and School Outcomes: A Systematic Review and Meta-Analysis of the Empirical Literature," *Review of Educational Research*, Vol. 89, No. 5, July 2019, pp. 785–827. As of May 14, 2020:
https://journals.sagepub.com/doi/abs/10.3102/0034654319866133

Lochmiller, Chad R., "Principal Coaching in Central Office Supervisory Roles: Exploring Persistent Tensions," *Voices of Reform: Educational Research to Inform and Reform*, Vol. 1, No. 1, September 2018, pp. 76–90. As of May 14, 2020:
https://www.voicesofreform.com/article/4488-principal-coaching-in-central-office-supervisory-roles-exploring-persistent-tensions

Louis, Karen Seashore, Kenneth Leithwood, Kyla L. Wahlstrom, Stephen E. Anderson, Michael Michlin, Blair Mascall, Molly Gordon, Tiiu Strauss, Emanda Thomas, and Shawn Moore, *Learning from Leadership: Investigating the Links to Improved Student Learning*, St. Paul, Minn.: University of Minnesota, July 2010. As of May 14, 2020:
https://conservancy.umn.edu/bitstream/handle/11299/140885/1/Learning-from-Leadership_Final-Research-Report_July-2010.pdf

Manna, Paul, *Developing Excellent School Principals to Advance Teaching and Learning: Considerations for State Policy*, New York, N.Y.: The Wallace Foundation, September 2015. As of May 14, 2020:
https://www.wallacefoundation.org/knowledge-center/pages/developing-excellent-school-principals.aspx

Marzano Research, website, undated. As of May 14, 2020:
https://www.marzanoresearch.com/

Marzano, Robert J., Timothy Waters, and Brian A. McNulty, *School Leadership That Works: From Research to Results*, Alexandria, Va.: Association for Supervision and Curriculum Development, September 2005.

National Policy Board for Educational Administration, website, undated. As of May 14, 2020:
http://npbea.org/

National Policy Board for Educational Administration, *Professional Standards for Educational Leaders*, Reston, Va., 2015. As of May 14, 2020:
http://www.npbea.org/wp-content/uploads/2017/06/Professional-Standards-for-Educational-Leaders_2015.pdf

Policy Studies Associates, *Principal Pipeline Self-Study Guide for Districts*, Washington, D.C., forthcoming (2020).

Robinson, Viviane M. J., Claire A. Lloyd, and Kenneth J. Rowe, "The Impact of Leadership on School Outcomes: An Analysis of the Differential Effects of Leadership Types," *Educational Administration Quarterly*, Vol. 44, No. 5, December 2008, pp. 635–674. As of May 14, 2020:
https://journals.sagepub.com/doi/10.1177/0013161X08321509

Scott, Deven, "50-State Comparison: School Leader Certification and Preparation Program," Education Commission of the States webpage, April 25, 2018. As of May 14, 2020:
https://www.ecs.org/50-state-comparison-school-leader-certification-and-preparation-programs/

Shelton, Sara, *Evaluating School Principals: A Legislative Approach*, Denver, Colo., and Washington, D.C.: National Conference of State Legislatures, May 2013. As of May 15, 2020:
https://www.ncsl.org/documents/educ/SchoolPrincipals.pdf

Stevens, David, and Jason Greenberg Motamedi, "Increasing Diversity in the Teacher Workforce: The Importance and Potential Impact of Authentic Change," webpage, February 8, 2019. As of May 15, 2020:
https://ies.ed.gov/ncee/edlabs/regions/northwest/blog/increasing-diversity.asp

Turnbull, Brenda J., Leslie M. Anderson, Derek L. Riley, Jaclyn R. MacFarlane, and Daniel K. Aladjem, *The Principal Pipeline Initiative in Action*, Washington, D.C.: Policy Studies Associates, Inc., PR-2445-WF, October 2016. As of May 15, 2020:
https://www.wallacefoundation.org/knowledge-center/pages/building-a-stronger-principalship-vol-5-the-principal-pipeline-initiative-in-action.aspx

U.S. Department of Education, *The State of Racial Diversity in the Educator Workforce*, Washington, D.C.: Policy and Program Studies Service, Office of Planning, Evaluation and Policy Development, July 2016. As of May 15, 2020:
https://www2.ed.gov/rschstat/eval/highered/racial-diversity/state-racial-diversity-workforce.pdf

Vanderbilt Assessment of Leadership in Education, website, undated. As of May 14, 2020:
https://valed.resonanteducation.com/

Wang, Elaine L., Susan M. Gates, Rebecca Herman, Monica Mean, Rachel Perera, Tiffany Berglund, Katie Whipkey, and Megan Andrew, *Launching a Redesign of University Principal Preparation Programs: Partners Collaborate for Change*, Santa Monica, Calif.: RAND Corporation, RR-2612-WF, 2018. As of May 15, 2020:
https://www.rand.org/pubs/research_reports/RR2612

Wildy, Helen, Coral Pepper, and Luo Guanzhong, "Applying Standards for Leaders to the Selection of Secondary School Principals," *Journal of Educational Administration*, No. 49, No. 3, May 2011, pp. 276–291. As of May 15, 2020:
https://www.emerald.com/insight/content/doi/10.1108/09578231111129064/full/html